Eternal Praise

By

Curtis Butler

Eternal Praise by Curtis Butler
Published by Austin Brothers Publishing
Fort Worth, TX
ISBN: 978-0-9964285-2-1

Scripture quotations taken from THE AMPLIFIED BIBLE (AMP), copyright © 1954, 1958, 1962, 1964, 1965, 1987 by the Lockman Foundation. All rights reserved. Used by permission. (www.Lockman.org).

Scripture quotations taken marked ESV are from The ESV® Bible (The Holy Bible, English Standard Version), copyright © 2001 by Crossway Bibles, a publishing ministry of Good News Publishers. Used by permission. All rights reserved.

Scripture quotations taken from The New American Standard Bible (NASB), copyright © 1960, 1962, 1963, 1968, 1971, 1972, 1973, 1975, 1977, 1995 by The Lockman Foundation. Used by permission.

Scripture quotations taken from the New King James Version (NKJV), copyright © 1979, 1980, 1982 by Thomas Nelson Inc. Used by permission. All rights reserved.

Scripture quotations taken from the Holy Bible New Living Translation (NLT), copyright © 1996. Used by permission of Tyndale House Publishers, Inc. Wheaton IL 60189. All rights reserved.

All rights reserved. No part of this publication may be reproduced, stored in a retrival system, or transmitted in any form or by an means—for example, electronic, photocopy, recording—without the prior written permission of the publisher. The only exception is brief quotations in printed reviews.

Copyright © 2015 - Curtis Butler

I dedicate my first book to my beloved mother, Idell Butler. Thank you Mom for allowing God to use you to lead me to the well of worship. At the well, I found a portal, which is the doorway that only true worshippers find, and are truly satisfied. Through your example I was able to see the window which leads one to eternal places, and brings the temporal face to face with the one and only true and living Eternal God.

Thanks Mom for keeping all us Butler kids in church, and for living a devoted life before us as a true-worshipper.

Thanks for the early years of inspiration, spiritual education, and the personal encouragement you gave. I've made so many mistakes along the way, but I've never veered away from the course you set me on many years ago.

Because of the seed you sowed in my heart, I am committed to spend the rest of my time, my talents, and my energy getting to know this eternal God you introduced to me. I will endeavor to use my gifts to present this eternal God to the hurting world.

Contents

Foreword	1
Introduction	3
Glimpse of the Eternal	7
A Taste of Eternity	15
Eternal Praise	21
God Is Eternal	29
The Praise of Men and of God	41
The Dead Don't Praise God	51
Don't Stop Praising	57
MY Testimony	65
Eternality of Words	73
Eternality Of Music	81
Eternal Warfare	93
In the Spirit, In the Eternal	103
Butler Ministries Resources	113
About the Author	117

Praise Songs

He Reigns	5
Worship You	12
Eternal Praise	19
Sacrifice	27
Jehovah-Shammah	37
Be Pleased	50
We Praise Your Name	55
Praise Is a Weapon	62
My Everything	79
Everything That Has Breath	85
Victory	100
Hiding Place	110

Foreword

Words cannot express the joy I have as a result of the release of this impartation to the Body of Christ. Curtis Butler is a modern-day David to this generation. He is a psalmist, worship leader, preacher, and pastor who has learned to use his prophetic praise as a weapon of warfare. He has truly captured the heart of God in *Eternal Praise*.

Curtis was ordained, like the prophet Jeremiah, before he was born, to release praise and worship to the Body of Christ. His life experiences and calling are his resume' and qualify him to speak on the subject of praise and worship. His written songs demonstrate his anointing for praise and worship. His knowledge and education affirm his passion for praise and worship. His longevity in ministry confirms his intimate knowledge of our Heavenly Father.

Eternal Praise is a clarion call in the Kingdom that summons believers to properly position themselves as worship-warriors. Your worship will be transformed as you read *Eternal Praise*. Curtis masterfully weaves a beautiful tapestry of worship with threads of theological constructs, Scripture, and songs of praise. You will feast on the spiritual meat of revelation regarding praise and worship. In addition, you will find yourself encountering our sovereign Lord, as Curtis ushers you into His presence with songs released from heaven's throne room.

I am honored and humbled that Curtis serves our local assembly as our pastor of worship. This book will transform your life. You will find an insatiable desire to get to know God like never before. God alone is truly worthy of *Eternal Praise*.

Patrick McGrew
Senior Pastor
Higher Praise Family Church

Introduction

Please allow me to begin our journey with prayer and praise:

Dear Heavenly Father, Creator of heaven and earth, to You I give the glory for the multiple things You have wrought in my life. If there be any good to come from my living, it is all because of You. Thank You for trusting me with this challenge, to write a book about something that is so dear to Your heart. My desire is to please You with every gift that You have given me. So let these few pages bring pleasure, first to You, then to every reader who picks it up to read.

Eternal God, I thank You for the opportunity to share with other worshippers this revelation and understanding of *Eternal Praise*. Eternal Spirit of God, please cause these words to illuminate in the hearts and minds of each person who reads, and cause the messages hidden within these pages to be revealed with clarity and accuracy. Let it be so that before the conclusion of this book there will be understanding, true transformation, and perpetual praise for You oh Lord God Almighty!

Oh God, please receive the praise interwoven throughout the pages of this book, and the praise offered by the readers. For Yours is the Kingdom, the power, and the glory. I declare now and forevermore that there is none like You, there is none to compare to You, and You are above all things because You reign. These things I pray in the powerful name of Jesus Christ, Your eternal Son, My eternal Savior. Amen!

Join me in praise with this song:

Eternal Praise

He Reigns

by Curtis L. Butler

Verse 1:

From the rising of the morning sun, to the going down of the same
Lord, You rule with great authority, and with sovereignty, You reign
Who can handle the perplexities that plague this human race
Who can stand Your awesomeness, as Your glory fills this place
Creation declares Your holiness with fire, wind and rain
It's You Who created the universe
Hallelujah! the Almighty reigns

Chorus:

Hallelujah! For the Lord our God, the Almighty reigns
Hallelujah! For the Lord our God, the Almighty reigns (repeat)

Verse 2:

It is You Who holds us gently in the palm of Your great hand
The earth will tremble and the mountains quake
At the sound of Your command
When foe and famine come our way with a flood of great disdain
And life so bitter strikes the heart with a paralyzing pain
Our lips will shout a heavenly chorus that our hearts cannot refrain
Heaven and earth will hear our praise hallelujah! the Almighty reigns

Chorus:

Hallelujah! For the Lord our God, the Almighty reigns
Hallelujah! For the Lord our God, the Almighty reigns

Bridge:

He reigns, He reigns, He reigns, the Almighty reigns (repeat)

Tag:

Hallelujah, hallelujah, hallelujah, Hallelujah, hallelujah, hallelujah
The Lord God omnipotent, He reigns forevermore, forevermore

As we move through these chapters, you will be invited to join in praise with the many who will be reading also. I will share original songs to assist you in doing so. Please do not let the songs limit your expressions of love to the Father. No matter whether you are loud and demonstrative, or silent before God, just be free in your worship to Him. As you embrace every opportunity to worship and praise in this book, please be sure that you worship in truth and in the spirit.

CHAPTER 1
Glimpse of the Eternal

For most of my life the Lord has been defining and redefining me as a music minister in the Body of Christ. I have always been a church goer since as young as I can remember. Going to church was fun for me because we lived in the country, northwest of Lubbock, Texas. Going to church provided something out of the ordinary for us to do with our time. I liked the singing, and I also enjoyed watching the preacher as he'd tune up to sing his sermons. All the people got happy and watching them react to the Holy Ghost was better than watching our little black and white television.

Another part of church that I enjoyed as a child was the music. Usually there was a beat up piano and a tambourine somewhere in the sanctuary. Some places we went to even had an organ.

I don't recall my dad going to church with us during early childhood, and when it came to people in general, he kept mostly to himself. It was later in life, after I was out of the house, that Dad started going to church, and actually got saved. Much like my grandma (Dad's mom), when Dad got saved, he was a beautiful person. I admired him because he was a hard working black man. As a child, what I remember most about my father is what my mother would share with us. She would always paint a vivid picture of dad as she told us stories of how they first met. Mom told us how he played the guitar and sang to her. Mom told us that Dad was a musician who had aspirations to someday be a high school band director. But life, as it was at that time, made it hard for a black man to go farther than a high school education. So he worked on cars, which he was another of his skills.

He also played the electric guitar like nobody I knew. Dad had a high pitched speaking and singing voice. I never knew him to play or sing in church, possibly because the electric guitar was early on labeled as the devil's instrument, and men with high pitched singing voices were not asked to lead songs in church. Most of my memories of Dad's musicianship were of him playing the blues on the front porch of our house. My oldest brother and I used to watch and marvel at Dad's ability with that electric guitar. Pretty soon he had multiple guitars, and he gave each of us one.

From that day on, we thought a lot about becoming famous musicians. I remember my brother Otis and me pretending to be the Beatles or the Jackson 5. We started out using sticks until Dad gave us real electric guitars. We formed our own little band in the 6th grade, and the music in us began to grow.

My mom, on the other hand, was not a musician; and even though she wasn't the best at it, she loved to sing. I suppose it was her relationship with God that I really admired. It was Mom who made every effort to keep all six children in church. She read stories from the Bible to us and teach us how to pray. I remember her kneeling all six or seven of us along the side of our bed and leading us in the Lord's Prayer. Mom would tell us how much God loved us and how we should love Him. She was the one person who taught me how to worship.

I remember, many times, Mom standing at the kitchen sink singing while washing dishes or at the oven cooking a meal. She would start out humming, which turned into singing and praying. The next thing I knew tears would be running down her face and dripping into the soapy water. Before long her hands would leave the dirty dish water and dishes to themselves, as she raised them up shouting "Lord, have mercy," and "Thank You, Jesus." At first I was worried for her, then I'd see a big smile on her face, which made me feel as if everything was ok.

With her eyes closed and hands raised, song after song kept ringing from her heart. She would pray and sing and cry till she was content. At times, I felt like I was with her, and neither of us was there in the kitchen anymore. We were in another place, the very presence of God. After a while Mom would turn around and catch me, her baby boy standing and staring in amazement! As a 5-year old I didn't fully understand it all, but I knew I wanted what my mom had. Little did I know this was my first glimpse of *Eternal Praise*.

Allow me to skip ahead in my story to my teens. At fifteen years old, I was saved and filled with the Holy Ghost. I decided I wanted to learn how to play the piano so I could use my music for God. At that time, guitars and drums were not accepted as part of our church worship. I started taking piano lessons and our church musician taught me how to play two or three songs.

By the time I was sixteen, I was playing the piano in our Sunday School, and by 19 I had become the Minister of Music at our Baptist church. With only a few songs and fewer chord progressions under my belt, I would teach harmony parts, and lead our adult sanctuary choir and youth/children's choir. Soon after I graduated from high school, I went to Junior College and took music theory, private voice, and piano. I joined every choir, every ensemble and singing group that I could get into. I wasn't the best musician around, but for all that I could not do with my voice and piano, I had plenty enough zeal to compensate.

I was radically saved and I wanted desperately to please God. Since I couldn't play every song I heard, and my reading skills were not fully developed, I began to write my own songs for church services. I would use the few chords I knew, the few scriptures I knew, and give it back to God; out of that came powerful songs that helped me grow over the years, and blessed the people of our congregation too. Before long, I began to hunger for God's presence like never before, so I would play my piano, sing, and cry (as my mother did) until my heart's content. This season in my life seems to have never ended, and even to this day I live to seek His presence.

Eternal Praise

Within these next few pages, I'd like to share my journey with you and hope you too will make our Eternal God and His Eternal presence your personal quest in life. My hope is that, as you read these few pages, you not only gain a greater insight that will strengthen your knowledge base in spiritual things, but that you will experience it eternally. Let's begin our walk with worship. Put this song on and sing along with it. If you do not have the recorded music, create your own melody with the words, and sing a new song to the Lord. Allow this worship song to assist you in kissing the Lord.

Curtis Butler

Worship You
by Curtis L. Butler

Verse 1:

I will sing of Your mercy, I will sing of Your grace

I will sing of Your love towards me

Till Your glory fills this place

Worship You, I will worship You

Worship You, I will worship You

Verse 2:

I will send a kiss towards You

With my whole heart I'll seek Your face

My soul has long a waited, just to meet with You this way

Worship You, I will worship You

Worship You, I will worship You

Chorus:

Till Your glory fills this temple

Till all darkness pass away

Worship You

I will lay myself before You

To be more like You I pray

Worship You

Tag:

I will worship You, I will worship

Eternal Praise

Take this moment to worship the Lord by sending kisses to him. As a child who would kiss Daddy on the jaw, you can kiss God with your worship. Worship implies relationship, and it signifies right relationship. Right now, with all your soul (your mind, your will, your emotions, and intellect) begin to brag on the Lord. Remind yourself of what He has done for you, your loved ones, and all humanity. Do your best to say what God means to you. He is so good and so worthy of our sincere worship. If you need to, please feel to sing the song again, and press into the eternal space of God.

CHAPTER 2
A Taste of Eternity

    I remember a very unusual Sunday morning for me. I did not go to my church on that specific Lord's day. I would never miss church! That's the way my Mom raised me, my one brother, and five sisters. We were always in a church. Sometimes it was Pentecostal, sometimes Methodist, and sometimes Church of God in Christ. Mom would send us, take us, and even drag us to any place that taught the Word of God. It depended on what church was closest to the house where we lived.

    Another reason I never missed church was that I was our church musician, and we had two services (sometimes three to four) every Sunday. I would play my piano and sing for every service, and I loved it! I don't remember the details or why, but I was given permission by my pastor to take a Sunday and get away. Although the time off was much appreciated, because my soul yearned for His presence, I ended up attending another church on that particular Sunday.

I found myself sitting with my wife, Laura. We sat in the back, worshipping with the largest congregation I had ever seen at that time in my life. It felt awkward for many reasons. Just to name a few, we were accustomed to being on the platform in charge of making things happen in the worship service. Another reason was the fact that we were the only couple of our ethnicity. The congregation was predominately white, but we tried to blend in as best we could.

I remember questioning myself, sarcastically, "Why are we here?" While sitting there, I felt strongly that God wanted to show us something. We were members of a Black Baptist church, and we had great singing, great preaching, and a great family of believers. I couldn't imagine what I could learn from this congregation that clapped on the one and three, and sang in octaves for most of their songs. But I was determined to be as open and optimistic as I possibly could.

After a while, people began gathering in front at the altar. The band played a simple progression of major chords while the people began to sing. No one sang the same words as the person next to them; in fact, they seemed to improvise as they lifted their voices in efforts to match the chord progressions produced by the band.

It wasn't long before I could hear the most beautiful sound I had ever heard. It sounded like thousands and thousands of angels singing along with the congregation. There was such an uninhibited freedom, and a definite indescribable unity in heart from every worshipper. Suddenly, the voices sounded like the thundering sound of a waterfall, or as scripture described it in Revelation, the sound of many rushing waters. It was as if God said "Hear my voice, and hear my praise." It was both frightening and inviting.

Laura and I stood to our feet, raising our hands, and lifting our voices in efforts to join this incredible sound. We entered into what we did not fully understand, we lost track of time, and found a door to an eternal place. I believe God made a deposit in me that day, which has taken me all these many years to really embrace. I'm still learning, and the more I learn the more I chase God for greater understanding. My life-long endeavor is to please Him in my worship and with my life. I don't recall if we ever visited the church again, but I had experienced worship from heaven. I guess you can say I had a taste of eternity.

The next Sunday we were back at our church having great services as usual, but I was never the same. I had tasted, heard, and seen too much. I was not fully content with the awesome church services that we experienced every week. No matter how high or how deep our worship services would get, I left service only partially satisfied. I knew there was something more, something deeper that God required of us, and I wanted to give it to Him.

There is a praise that invites heaven into the room, and that kind of atmosphere makes God feel at home. This kind of praise is as eternal as God himself, and this kind of praise belongs to God alone.

Through the pages of this book you will be encouraged to listen and to sing the songs given to me by the Holy Spirit. I ask that you pray that the Holy Spirit will help me to clearly articulate in these few chapters so that we gain a deeper understanding of the eternal praise and develop a burning desire to produce it for He who alone deserves it. Our eternal God deserves our eternal praise. Close your eyes, listen, sing, and worship our eternal God with this song.

Eternal Praise

by Curtis L. Butler

Intro:

(Ooh, ahh, worthy, worthy, worthy worthy)

You are worthy of all glory honor and power

For You have created all things

And for Your pleasure they were created

You are worthy of eternal praise

You are worthy of eternal praise

Verse 1:

All creation was created by Your hand

All that was and is and ever will be

Is a part of Your master plan

To replace the vacancy around heavens throne

To insure Your praises will go on, and on, and on, and on

Chorus:

We sing holy, holy, holy, holy Lord

Holy, holy, holy, holy Lord

You are worthy of eternal praise

You are worthy of eternal praise

Verse 2:

Twenty-four elders and four beasts bowing down

The true worshipers will lead the angelic host in a joyful sound

With one great voice we worship Your holy name

Casting down our golden crowns
We give You praise, praise, praise, praise

Chorus:

We sing holy, holy, holy, holy Lord
We sing holy, holy, holy, holy Lord
You are worthy of eternal praise
You are worthy of eternal praise.

Tag:

(Kadosh, kadosh, kadosh
Adonai, Elohim, zet viot, ashe ayah, ve hove, ve yavo!)
Holy, holy, holy, Lord God Almighty
Which was and is and is to come! Is to come

During your time of worship, read and meditate on Revelation chapter four. Try to see yourself there, engaged in the heavenly worship that takes place in John's vision.

CHAPTER 3
Eternal Praise

When we look at the word *eternal*, we can't help but to say… "Wow"! What a concept to try to understand; that we, finite creatures, are invited to know and understand the infinite. Eternal Life, Eternal God, Eternal Weight of Glory, these are words that we often hear and use as we speak the church language; but what does *eternal* mean, and what definition does it give the words life, God, and glory?

Without getting into the etymology of the word, we can simply and safely say that *eternal* means to last forever, never coming to an end. Webster says, *eternal* is "to exist with no beginning and no end; unending, meant to last indefinitely." We know this also because God is Who He is, man had to come up with a word to describe Him. God was eternal way before we conjured up the word *eternal* (Deuteronomy 33:27).

We are equipped to do many wonderful things with our minds, bodies, spirits, talents, and time; but if we are not bringing glory and honor to God with them, we are not fulfilling our purpose in life, and neither are we fulfilled. We are created to show forth the praises of Him Who called us out of darkness into His marvelous light (1 Peter 2:9).

Let's not waste any more of our precious time, but spend the rest of our lives giving continual praise to the eternal God. When we praise Him, He shows up, bringing with Him all of His goodness, grace, and mercy. His presence is His favor on our lives. I want to praise Him right now, but before I do, let me reiterate and make it clear that God alone has exclusive rights to the praise that never ends! We recognize the eternalness of God when we praise Him without ceasing. All creation exists to bring glory to our eternal Creator.

The Psalmist says all creation declares the glory of God.

"Praise Him, sun and moon; praise Him all you shining stars!
Praise Him you highest heavens and you waters above the heavens.
Praise the Lord from the earth, you sea monsters and all deeps,
Fire and hell, snow and mist, stormy wind, fulfilling His Word!
Mountains and all hills, fruit trees and all cedars!
Let them praise the name of the Lord for His name alone is exalted;
His majesty is above earth and heaven."
(Ps. 148:3-4, 7-9, 13 ESV)

When we think about it, creation never stops praising God. When men close their mouths, when laws and decrees dictate that we should not praise God, creation still shows forth His glorious power.

Eternal Praise

Winter, spring, summer, and fall, creation never ceases bringing glory to its Creator God. Throughout every generation, man has been able to look at creation in awe of its splendor and concluding there must be a Supreme Designer who exists above and beyond us all. We too should be as consistent in our praise of God. Our resolve should be that of David who was determined to bless the Lord at all times with a continual praise in his mouth (Psalm 34:1).

We too can produce an eternal praise, a praise that never stops, but goes on and on. You might ask how. Well there are several ways, if we think about it. One is by allowing our lives to do the praising. Far too often we limit our praise to what we can do with our lips. Consequently, we run out of words. Many times when I'm speaking or singing of Gods worth, I can't find the words to adequately reveal what I feel. Sometimes the words I find take away from what I really mean to say. I can't count how many hours I spend trying to find the words I need to express a song that I am writing. Even this book has presented me with the same challenge. So I've had to study more words, and take multiple mental breaks along the way, in search of words I could use to communicate exactly what I want to say.

Let's remember Revelation 4:11 which states that God created all things because it brought Him pleasure. In Genesis, God declared that all He had created was good to Him. It pleased God because it was good, and it was good because He made it. We bring glory to God by being exactly what He created us to be, and by doing what He created us to do. Because God created Adam, He was pleased with him and was glorified in that alone. And when God told Adam to be fruitful and multiply, as long as Adam did that, He brought glory to God.

We have to understand that our existence, just as the stars in the heavens, brings glory and honor to God. Just by shinning, the stars are praising God. Did you know that even in the light of the bright sunshine the stars are yet shinning? Even though we can't see their glittering light with the natural eye, they continually shine. Just because God created us, He loves us and finds pleasurable praise in that alone. There is nothing more we need to do in order to glorify God. Our all-wise Creator has formed and fashioned us to produce perpetual praise for Himself.

When we fulfill the God-given purpose for us in life, we bring glory to Him. Let's look at one of the purposes of God for us in 1 Peter 2:9.

But you are a chosen people, and a royal priesthood, a holy nation, God's special possession, that you may declare the praises of Him Who called you out of darkness into His wonderful light. (NIV)

God has chosen us to be a royal priesthood, a holy nation, and called us out of darkness for the purpose of declaring His praises. When we declare His praises, we are fulfilling His purpose for calling us out of darkness; consequently, we bring glory and honor to God. As believers we have been chosen by God to praise Him. We are not saved to simply miss out on the horrors of a very real hell, but we are saved to praise our God.

A royal priesthood (*hierateuma* describes a priestly fraternity) is a group assigned a specific job, which held certain responsibilities and privileges. In the Old Testament times, a priest was called and anointed to serve the people, especially in worship ceremonies. The priest had to offer sacrifices to atone for the sins of the people.

Now, in the New Testament era, the believer is able to go before God without a mediator or a priest, because we have been chosen by God to be part of a royal priesthood. The veil has been split in half from top to bottom (Matthew 27:51), and we can boldly go directly to our Father in prayer, and in worship. Our High Priest is Jesus Christ, Who first shed His life blood to pay the price for man's sin, past, present, and future. And now, Jesus is at the right hand of the Father in heaven, and intercedes for us (Hebrews 7:25).

As part of His priesthood, we can join in with Christ, through the Holy Spirit, in prayer and intercession. Since the ultimate sacrifice has been made, there is no more need for a blood sacrifice. We now offer unto God a sacrifice of praise.

Through Jesus, therefore, let us continually offer to God a sacrifice of praise…the fruit of lips that openly profess His name. (Hebrews 13:15 NIV)

Scripture says we should offer a sacrifice of praise continually. This means without ceasing. Our sacrifice of praise is an eternal praise, because it should happen in and out of every season of our lives. The sacrificial praise means to have an attitude of gratefulness toward God, in spite of our situations and circumstances. In order for our sacrifice of praise to be ongoing, it must become eternal before God. We should have a continual attitude of thanksgiving toward God. Let's take this moment to offer to our God the sacrifice of praise with this song:

Eternal Praise

Sacrifice

by Curtis L. Butler

Chant:

I've got something for You, bring it on. Ah yeah, sacrifice

We've got something for You, bring it on. Ah huh, ah huh, sacrifice

I've got something for You, bring it on. Are You ready for this, sacrifice

We've got something for You, bring it on. Hear we go, hear we go

Chorus:

We bring the sacrifice into the house of the Lord

We bring the sacrifice into the house of the Lord

Verse 1:

It doesn't matter how you feel

You just need to know the Lord is really real

One day He paid the price the greatest sacrifice

The least that you and I can do is lift our voice and say thank You

Thank You! (4x's)

Verse 2:

You might be rich you, might be poor

But you've got something you can give to the Lord

If God's been good to you, done anything for you

The least that you and I can do

Is lift our voice and say thank You

Thank You! (4x's)

We bring the sacrifice into the house of the Lord
We bring the sacrifice into the house of the Lord

Bridge:

And we offer up to You the sacrifices of thanksgiving
And we offer up to You the sacrifice
The sacrifice, the sacrifice, the sacrifice
Bring it on, sacrifice
Bring it on, sacrifice
Bring it on, sacrifice
Bring it on

Rap:

Do you wanna sacrifice, really wanna sacrifice
Bring it to God if you do it right
Won't you lay your burdens on the table 'cause you know He's able
My God comes right back 'cause He's stable
(Do you want to sacrifice, really want to sacrifice
Do you really, really want to sacrifice?)
We bring the sacrifice, we bring the sacrifice, we bring the sacrifice of praise

In the Old Testament the priests were to make blood sacrifices daily for the sins of the people as well as for themselves. We, as members of a royal priesthood, are to bring a continual sacrifice of praise. Our sacrifice is not to cover sins to appease a holy God, but to applaud an all-wise, merciful God. We praise God, because through His Son, Jesus Christ, He has taken away the sins of the world.

CHAPTER 4
God Is Eternal

When I think of eternal, I automatically think of God. All other things, if anything else, that would fit this description must find its origin in God. Nothing can give a purer definition of the word *eternal* than God Himself. As we come to understand God, we can better understand the concept of eternal.

Throughout these few pages, I may use the word eternal to describe God, but the actual truth is that God is the description and the true definition of eternal. Allow me to pause to state a few facts about God; just a few things I've learned in this short life. First of all, God has no beginning, because He is the beginning of all things. God has no end because He is the end of all things. Genesis 1 says, "In the beginning God created the heavens and the earth"…this reveals that even before the beginning began, God existed. In Revelation 22:13 (KJV), the Son of God declares it like this: I am the Alpha and Omega, the beginning and the end, the first and the last."

He lives outside of time, and is not confined to its limitations. God is the beginning of all things, the end of all things. And when all else comes to its end, God still is. No one else can claim ownership to these communicable attributes except Yahweh, the eternal God.

Psalm 102:25-27 (ESV) states: "Of old, You laid the foundation of the earth, and the heavens are the work of Your hands. They will perish, but You will endure; they will wear out like a garment. You change them like a robe, and they will pass away; but You are the same and Your years have no end."

God is therefore eternal without beginning, without end, and must receive eternal praise. This characteristic of God is called an *incommunicable attribute* of God according to Wayne Grudem's Systematic Theology. Allow me to add this statement; everything that is eternal is like God. It is not God nor is it equal to God, but it is like Him in an eternal sense.

All that is like Him rightfully belongs to Him, because it comes from Him. God is the Father of all that possess the eternal traits. For instance, the wind is not God, but it is like God. We can't mark its beginning point with our natural eye, nor can we determine with accuracy its ending destination. Furthermore, we don't see the wind, but we are certain of its reality because we feel it brush against our sensitive skin, and we see the trees bend in its passing. The wind is invisible, but it possesses great power over creation. It produces tornadoes, hurricanes, tsunamis, and all kinds of deadly storms, but the wind is not God, only it is like God in this attribute.

The Holy Spirit is thought to be the Breath or the Wind of God. Just like the wind, you can't see God or the Holy Spirit, but you can see evidence of His presence. All creation speaks of its Creator God. The omnipotent God has great power over all creation. It is He who sends the wind with the blast of His nostrils. It is God who sends the rain and causes the waters to rise and fall. He alone orchestrates the symphony of life on earth, and directs the course of human history. We may not be able to see Him, but we can trace His footsteps and find His fingerprints in our lives.

It should bring comfort to us to know that God reigns over all mankind, and the affairs of every nation. Life can seem dark and hopeless, leaving us in fear of what could happen next, but when we remind ourselves that a loving, all-powerful God is in control, we find a reason to smile, sing, and carry on.

Let us further note that it is the eternalness of God that sets Him apart, and above all other beings. God alone can bear the weight of this title. All the great men and women who have lived on this earth have come to a definite end. And all the momentous events that have taken place have faded as time passed. If they are remembered, it is in less vivid details than when they happened. The most brilliant secular minds, the most devout atheist, the most lasting religions of all kinds, and even our world's system have tried in every generation to erase God from society, only to find that it just doesn't happen. God's existence will never fade, and why? Because He is eternal, and He has no end. His reputation is eternal. Evidence of His presence has been seen in every creature since the beginning of recorded time.

"…I am the Alpha, the Omega, the Beginning and the End…" These words are declared by the Lord Himself (Revelation 22:13), He says, "I am the Alpha and the Omega." Notice, He did not say He was an Alpha and an Omega, a beginning and an end, because there is none like Him. There is only one first and one last, no one can share this title, only one Person. That Person is the Triune Hebrew God, Elohim!

The words *Alpha* and *Omega* are the first and last letters of the Greek alphabet, and they simply mean that God is the beginning of everything; He is before everything, and the origin of everything. He is the end or the goal of everything; the purpose of everything, and the conclusion of all that has ever existed. The Person who holds this title has no choice but to be eternal in nature.

We cannot go back far enough to find the moment that God was born, because He has no date of birth; nor can we be transported so far enough into the future that we can witness the funeral services of our unending God. In Job 36:26 (ESV), Elihu says of God, "…the number of your years is unsearchable." This knowledge alone should make us lift our hands in praise to the Eternal God. He did not begin like us, and is superior to any of us, deserving recognition as the only sovereign Eternal God.

Wayne Grudem states that, "God has no beginning, end, or succession of moments in His own being." He goes on to say that, "God sees all time equally and vividly, yet He sees events in time and acts in time." (Systematic Theology, pg. 168)

The more we come to know God, the more we will praise Him, which transforms our momentary praise into continuous, perpetual praise. It should be with every heartbeat and with every breath we take that we find reason to give God praise. Yes, the kind of praise that goes on and on. This kind of praise is called eternal praise. The Scriptures declare…

> *…to Him (God) belongs eternal praise. (Psalm 111:10b, NIV parenthetic insertion mine)*

In other words, it is God who holds claim to the praise that will never end. And He is the rightful owner of the eternal praise. It belongs to Him alone.

Praise means to speak well of; *eternal praise* means to speak well of without ceasing. This kind of praise is ascribed only to Jehovah; not Buddha, Mohammed, Krishna, or any other religious person or deity. These worshipped beings, and all who will follow them, quickly fade in luster when compared to God Almighty.

Even God proclaims Himself to be one of a kind, and that there is no one like Him. When we read Isaiah 46:9-10, God says it this way;

> *I am God, there is none like Me, declaring the end from the beginning and from ancient times things not yet done, saying My counsel shall stand, and I will accomplish all My purpose… (ESV)*

God says He is God, and there is none like Him. Though He made us in His image and likeness, we cannot be equal to Almighty God. We have a definite beginning and end that separates us, and makes God holy and unique. God is seated high above us with all power and authority. In this passage of scripture God points out that He declares what the end is going to be from the beginning. We as human beings fall short in this regard.

The Mayans were a primitive Indian culture mainly of the Yucatan, British Honduras, Guatemala, and the state of Tabasco, Mexico. Their common language was Mayan, and they predicted the end of all mankind. Their doomsday proclamation was to occur December 21, 2012. Many people believed, and others wondered if they were accurate in their prophecy, but it turned out that they were wrong. Others have tried to calculate and prophecy the end of time only to be embarrassed in their predictions. According to scripture, God alone can declare the end from the beginning. Only He can declare a thing ancient when it first begins. His counsel stands in every culture, in every generation, in all times.

Let me note that you and I have our own fingerprint, and no one else in the world has one like it. It identifies us and distinguishes us from all others who resemble us. There are things that set God apart from all else, as if it were His own fingerprint. Eternal praise is one of those things. Just as our individual fingerprint belongs to us and no one else, so does eternal praise belong to God and no one else.

Eternal praise identifies God, and distinguishes Him from all else. There may be those who call themselves a god, and might act like a god, but they are not God. They may deserve praise for great acts and noble accomplishments, but the eternal praise does not belong to them! I can't say it enough, so I'll state it again, eternal praise belongs to God, and God alone. All creation must come to this realization, and all creation must raise an unending sound that declares Gods superiority over the universe and its inhabitants.

Let's look deeper at the eternalness of God. God is infinite and unlimited by the confines of time. The Bible speaks of the eternality of God in Ps. 90:2:

Before the mountains were born or You gave birth to the earth and the world, even from everlasting to everlasting you are God.
(NASB)

God speaks through David the Psalmist who said that God gave birth to the mountains and brought forth the earth and the world that we now know. This makes God the parent of all creation. It is common knowledge that our parents exist years before our conception. And they know more about us than we know about ourselves. We must trust them to take care and provide all our needs.

It puzzles me why we can acknowledge our earthly parents as worthy of our respect and honor, but it is foreign for us to see God in this manner. Consequently, we fail to give Him due respect, honor and praise. It was God who gave birth to all who live, even those who choose to close their eyes to His reality. Our Father God gives us breath, and a sense of being. As our spiritual parent, He protects us from seen and unseen dangers. God provides the basic needs of every human being, and God determines the day we live and the day we die. He existed before us and will exist after we pass on, because He has no beginning and no end. Look at this next scripture:

For thus says the High and Lofty One, who inhabits eternity, whose name is Holy: 'I dwell in the high and holy place, with him who has a contrite and humble spirit, to revive the spirit of the humble, and to revive the heart of the contrite ones.' (Isaiah 57:15 NKJV)

God says of Himself that He is high and holy, that He lives in a holy place with a holy name, but at the same time He lives with us who are lowly in heart and contrite in spirit. He then is here with us and there in a holy place reserved for Him. God is present at the highest and lowest places all at once. What a declaration! One of the Hebrew names of God is Jehovah-Shammah, which is interpreted as "God Is Present." Wayne Grudem's Systematic Theology would refer to this attribute as omnipresent. I know of no other deity that can lay such claim.

From this knowledge I was inspired to write a song to celebrate the omnipresence of God. As the Psalmist David would say, "Oh magnify the Lord with me, let us exalt His name together" (Psalm 34:3, NKJV). His name is Jehovah-Shammah.

Eternal Praise

Jehovah-Shammah
by Curtis L. Butler

Verse:

Jehovah-Shammah, our God is everywhere
Where can we go to find that He's not there
The highest mountain, the lowest valley tells
There is no place where His power is not felt

Chorus:

Celebrate the presence of our God
For in His presence our joy is fulfilled
Come now before Him with music and singing
And dancing as His glory is now revealed

Bridge:

Jehovah-Shammah, in every place there is on earth
Jehovah-Shammah, at the farthest ends of the universe
Jehovah-Shammah, in the palace halls of the Kings
Jehovah-Shammah, where the worshipers are worshipping
Jehovah-Shammah, where the little boys and girls are living in the streets
Jehovah-Shammah, in the wind that blows and in the air we breathe
Jehovah-Shammah, on the mountains high and the valleys low
Jehovah-Shammah, He's omnipotent and everywhere we go

(Rap by Adrion Butler):

I call Him Jehovah-Shammah, top of the game like Barak Obama,

He's in the mix so there is no drama;
He's bigger than the rest like an anaconda,
And I meant that, I serve Him like a cadet,
He is everywhere and it's impossible for me to miss it.
So why would I lie, acuna-ma-tata,
Cause when I'm in His will my worries go bye-bye;
Sayonara and adios, I'm in the middle of a storm
so I keep Him close; when most of my friends leave
And they catch ghost like Michael Phelps
In a hundred breast-strokes,
But they wasn't and it was obvious;
Money is finally right cause in God we trust
And He's everywhere like a transit bus,
He's a natural high no cannabis.

Tag:

Jehovah-Shammah, Jehovah-Shammah, He's here!
Jehovah-Shammah!

It should bring comfort to know that wherever you are in life, God is there. In times of sorrow, He's there to bring comfort. In times of prosperity, He's present to bring wisdom and balance. I've seen God in the midst of a congregation when everyone in the building was slain in His presence, and I've seen Him in the kitchen with my mother, with tears running down her face, while she was cooking biscuits and homemade syrup for seven hungry children. He is in my past watching over me, in my future sustaining me, and in my present ordering my footsteps, all at the same instant. I know it's difficult to wrap our little brain around all that, but it is still truth. Let's read Gen.1:1-5,14-18 (KJV):

> *In the beginning God created the heavens and the earth. And the earth was without form and void; and darkness was upon the face of the deep. And the Spirit of God moved upon the face of the waters.*
> *And God said 'Let there be light': and there was light. And God saw the light that it was good; and God divided the light from the darkness. And God called the light day and the darkness He called night. And the evening and the morning was the first day.*
> *And God said 'Let there be lights in the firmament of the heaven to divide the day from the night, and let them be for signs, and for seasons, and for days and years:*
> *And let them be for lights in the firmament of the heaven to give light upon the earth'; and it was so.*
> *And God made two great lights, the greater light to rule the day, and the lesser light to rule the night, He made the stars also.*
> *And God set them in the firmament of the heaven to give light upon the earth, and to rule over the day and over the night, and to divide the light from the darkness; and God saw that it was good.*

Here in Genesis 1, as Creator, God brought everything into being. It is recorded that He initiates time, and he regulates time by alternating the light and darkness, by which He establishes the seasons, thereby bringing chronological order to chaos. We must understand that it is He who governs time, and all that exists within time.

Another of Gods incommunicable attributes is His ability to live outside of time and move within time. If you could do this, I'd gladly give you the eternal praise. We can only exist within time or outside of time, one place or the other. I am either at home in bed, or I am at *Six Flags Over Texas*, but I am not at both places at the same time. I am either 5 years old, with no cares in life, or I'm 45 years old, with the responsibilities of a CEO of a large company; but I can't be both at the same time. I can't live fully in the spirit and fully in my flesh at the same time, hence the battle that we all must fight. We can only exist in our seasons and times. Someday we will all exist outside of time, either eternally in heaven or eternally in hell. And so God will bring an end to time as we know it, according to His purposes and His sovereign will.

CHAPTER 5
The Praise of Men and of God

We often give praise to people for some good deed toward us or toward humanity; and it's ok to give credit to whom credit is due. When someone does well, we happily shower them with words of adoration and appreciation. Man was created to praise and will do it naturally. We praise our children for making good grades, and we praise our heroes who have given their lives for worthy causes. It is only natural and it is only right. It's in our DNA to praise, and it is God who put it there.

We need to also realize that God himself is a praiser; so one of our godly traits is to praise. You might ask the question, if God is a praiser, who would He praise? It's a reasonable question. Who is worthy of God's praise when the Bible makes it clear that we have all fallen short of the glory of God? There is no one higher than God, holier than God, or mightier than God. Who is worthy of a God-size praise?

I am uncomfortable when people praise me for something I do well. I try to be careful to thank them, and quickly direct the glory to God. Because of this uneasiness, I try to give people the right dose of praise, not an overdose.

It's been stated already that to praise is to speak well of. Therefore, if God is a praiser, He must find someone or something of which to speak well. Let's look at just a few times in scripture where God praised.

In the book of Genesis, God creates the heavens and the earth. During His creating, He would take praise breaks to say what He thought of His creation. After careful inspection of what was created, God's expressed the opinion that it was good. God has an opinion, and He is not afraid to express it.

We too should express our opinion of what God has done. After close examination of His goodness toward us, we should conclude that God is very good. We don't keep our opinion to ourselves, but we vocalize it. Let it be known, without reservation, our opinion of God and His mighty works in our life. Since we are created in God's likeness, we should be like Him, and in agreement with Him. Let's read this next scripture and see what there is to discover about our God as a praiser.

> *Now there was a day when the sons of God came to present themselves before the Lord, and Satan came also among them. And the Lord said unto Satan, 'Whence comest thou?' Then Satan answered the Lord, and said, 'From going to and fro in the earth,*

and from walking up and down it.' And the Lord said unto Satan, 'Hast thou considered my servant Job, that there is none like him in the earth, a perfect and upright man, one that feareth God, and escheweth evil?' (Job 1:6-8, KJV)

Listen to God brag on Job to the devil. He says consider my servant Job, there is nobody like him in all the earth. God proclaimed, as far as humans are concerned, Job was perfect, and always did what was right before the Lord. Job, according to God, demonstrated qualities that no other human had at this time. God did not say there are just a few like Job, but there was nobody like Job in all the earth. Now that will mess with your theology. By setting Job apart from all other men in the earth, God has dubbed his servant holy, and sacred. I could preach some more on this, but I will go on with my original point.

Note also the passage of scripture uses the word *fear*. Used here, it is the same as the word *worship* in the Hebrew mind of that day. So God says that Job is a worshiper, and that he abstains from evil doings. In other words, God spoke highly of Job in the presence of Satan and the sons of God, which were probably the angels. God the Son and the Holy Spirit were present as well, and everyone heard the praises of God.

Now let's rush past other men like Abraham, Moses, David, (and I know I'm missing others) and let's stop in the new testament to once more hear praise come from Gods mouth.

And Jesus, when He was baptized, went up straightway out of the water: and lo, the heavens were opened unto Him, and He saw the Spirit of God descending like a dove, and lighting upon Him: And lo a voice from heaven, saying, 'This is my beloved Son, in Whom I am well pleased.' (Matthew 3:16-17 KJV)

In this passage, God uses sight and sound to announce His praise. The Holy Spirit was there in the form of a dove to witness and agree with the Father's praise. John the Baptist, and all who were there at the Jordan River that day, heard the audible voice of God and saw this fantastic display of praise. It was with undeniable proclamation that God said "this is My Son, whom I love and, with whom, I am well pleased."

Remember praise means "to speak well of." Allow me to state it again, God is a praiser, and we who are created in His image and likeness are also praisers. One day, we as believers will anticipate the ultimate praise of God, when He speaks His opinion of us. He will say "Well done, my good and faithful servant…" (Matthew 25:23).

We should desire this eternal praise of God more than the temporal praise of men. Those who would be satisfied with the adoration and praise of men are like the one who finds ultimate satisfaction in the gift of one meal versus the gift of a job to generate many satisfying meals. The praise of men would last but a lifetime, but the praises of God gives life everlasting.

So again, God is a praiser, and has created and fashioned us to do likewise. We will praise someone for something because it's what we are wired to do. Since it is what we will do, we need to be careful about what and who we praise. More importantly, let us be mindful what kind of praise we attribute to whom.

Since we now know that God Himself is a praiser, and He praises us for the good that we do, we have to choose which praise we want more. Do you want the praise of God or the praises of men? The praise that comes from men is temporary, and too much of it can make you go mad. Much of our praise toward one another is exaggerated, and in some cases, tied to ulterior motives. The praise of God is eternal; it builds you up and prods you toward greatness.

Men only see the outward deeds of another and deem that person worthy of praise. God sees the inward and outward, the good and the bad part of us (1 Samuel 16:7) and His opinion of us is that we are the righteousness of God in Christ Jesus (2 Corinthians 5:21). God's opinion of us comes from what He knows of us in light of what Christ has done for us.

It blows me away that no matter how far I fall from grace, God's opinion does not change. I am convinced that God knows something that I don't know about me and my destiny. He tells me that I am an overcomer through Christ (Romans 8:37; Revelation 12:11). I look forward to God's ultimate praise, when He says "Well done my good and faithful servant." He will praise me before all of heaven, and say that I am good, a benefit to the Kingdom. He will affirm that I am faithful, and that I served Him well (Matthew 25:23). It doesn't matter what anyone else has to say about me on that day, I just want to hear God's praise when He looks at me.

But we must remember there is one kind of praise reserved for the only one, true, and living God, and that is the eternal praise. What happens when we give continual praise, or eternal praise, to human beings? The very thing that happens to kings, rulers, and pharaohs—they soon go mad. We are not designed to receive unending praise.

Personally, I have to keep myself on the altar before God, because as a worship leader I am before people weekly, singing and playing my instrument. I have to dress nice; I have to make my presentation as appealing as possible. Consequently, there's not a week that goes by that I don't receive a compliment, a word of encouragement, and/or praise from people. I can't afford not to take that praise and give it to God every time, because if I don't, then pride could easily sneak in and find root in my heart.

I am then in the same predicament as Lucifer who was created perfect, and the sin of iniquity was found in him. Lucifer's sin was pride. Pride made him believe he was equal to God and desired his own throne, where he would be worshipped like the Most High (Isaiah 14:12-14). I see it all the time in the lives of famous performers, musicians, actors, visual artists, dancers, and all sorts of successful/beautiful people. It doesn't matter if they are secular or Christian, the results are the same. What starts out good, clean, and wholesome turns out distorted, wicked, and evil. No matter how humble we see ourselves, praise that rightfully belongs to God, will ruin us.

As we look down the corridors of human history, we see that men have always built monuments for praise to worthy people. We have written books about them, and sang beautiful songs in memory of them. Praise comes so natural for us that we even give praise to our pets for obeying us. But that type of praise changes with every fleeting moment. As soon as the person we esteemed so highly falls short of our expectations, or the dog disobeys our command, that is where our praise ends.

This kind of praise, though notable, is not adequate for a God who never changes, a God who never diminishes in power. Our God never stops being great, He never stops being incredible; God never stops being sovereign, and He never stops being worthy of the highest praise. Therefore, as true worshipers, we must resolve in our inner most being to produce a worthy praise for a worthy God. The Psalmist David said in Psalm 34:1, "I will bless the Lord at all times and His praise shall continually be in my mouth." (NKJV)

For those of us who can only praise God when we feel those *Holy Ghost doodads*, you must know that this is not eternal praise. You may be one of those praisers who praises best when it's your favorite song being played, or your favorite worship leader leading worship service. Some praise best when the music is perfect, and those leading you in worship sing with perfect pitch.

I believe God grants us those worship services where the band misses its queues, the sopranos go flat on their high notes, and the worship leader has an off day, where he or she seemingly misses the leading of the Holy Spirit. I believe we have to sing songs that are not our all-time-favorites, or songs we don't know well, just to see if we will yet praise Him.

I've met those worshipers who can't see the eternal God because of the temporal humanness of others. But we must do as David did—engage his will. David's *want to* was the driving force of his praise to God.

Our praise quickly fades when we don't will to praise, because there will be opposition, distractions, and discouragements. Some days, you will have to press through to get to the place where your praise can actually flow. Our enemy does not want us to praise God, and certainly not for a lengthy time. We were created to praise God, we were born to bring God pleasure, and we exist to give Him glory (Colossians 1:16).

Now I've met those church folks who praise God on Sunday and curse like the devil Monday through Saturday. These praisers cannot produce the eternal praise that God requires. How can bitter and sweet water come from the same well (James 3:8-11)?

Maybe you don't use profanity, but you do say things that are not true, or speak slanderous words against someone; from your mouth comes bitter waters. If only we'd learn to praise instead of slander, speak words that bring glory to God and edify people. Try to find something good to say.

I've seen singers whose vocal skills were so incredible that the whole house screamed with applause. I've marveled at the musicians who played with such unlimited ability that you can't see God because of their gift. Onlookers fill the room with ecstatic praise, but not for God, the Giver of the gift. Often, I've wanted to be like them. Many times I felt like I had nothing to offer God. But I noticed that people would praise the gifted ones; however, nothing went to God.

Now in my later years, I just want to please God with my praise. I want my praise to be eternal, to rise higher than the church ceiling, to go beyond the moment, and last longer than the song. My prayer is that my expression of praise will always come from my heart, my inner man, the invisible part of me, my spirit, because God is Spirit; and that the words of my praise will always come from an overflow of the word of God, because they that worship Him must worship Him in spirit and in truth (John 4:23-24).

It should be that with every heartbeat, and with every breath we take, we would find reason enough to praise God. In every season of our lives, in every stage of our growth, in our mountain-top experiences and in the valleys, no matter how low, we have to praise God. David modeled this with his life. From shepherd boy to aged king, and all the days in between, David praised God. He sang in the solitude of dead nights while the sheep soundly slept. He praised God in the palace halls of a mad king, while deadly spears swooshed by his head. David gave praise to God while running and hiding as a forsaken fugitive; misunderstood and without understanding, he praised God.

I am amazed that with an empty stomach and aching muscles, he managed to tune out the present woes and worship God. He learned to lay aside his sword, and pick up his lyre to offer a love song to his Eternal God. As David did, we as true worshipers of God must also learn to offer Him Eternal Praise.

Curtis Butler

Be Pleased

by Curtis L. Butler

Be pleased, oh Lord, be pleased with the love that we bring You
Be pleased, oh Lord our God, with our worship
Be pleased with the song that we sing
Be pleased with the praise that we offer
Be pleased as we bow down before You in worship

For we know that all that we are is all that You want
Our bodies, our spirit, our soul
Our lives, our talents, our all we give to You right now

Give me the words and music
And I will bless You with wonderful praise
Anoint me afresh with Your Holy Spirit
And I will bring a smile to Your beautiful face

Be pleased, oh Lord
Be pleased with the love that we bring You
Be pleased, oh Lord our God, with our worship

Oh Lord, just be pleased,
Be pleased, be pleased, as we render our praise
Be pleased, be pleased, oh Lord, we pray.

CHAPTER 6
The Dead Don't Praise God

We must realize our praises should never cease. Even when we have every justifiable reason to close our eyes to God's goodness, and shut tight our lips in silence, we should always muster up praise for our very worthy God. This is the best time to shout with the voice of triumph (Psalm 47:1), to sing a song of praise, and bless the Lord with the fruit of our lips (Hebrews 15:13). Of course you know that when we refuse to praise God, in His eyes we are as dead men. The Bible says that the dead don't praise God. "The dead do not praise the Lord, nor any who go down into silence" (Psalm 115:17, NKJV).

Dead people can't see because their eyes are shut. They cannot feel, because their senses are numb to every sensation. The dead do not speak, and have no voice to cry, sing, shout, or mumble. They can't respond or react to anything that goes on around them, or happens to them. The scary thing is we imitate the dead when we choose to be silent rather than give God praise.

Have you sat beside the person in church worship service who chose not to respond in praises to God? While the truth is being preached, a powerful testimony is given, or the house is filled with Gods presence; they sit quietly, unmoved and untouched. I wonder if they've even heard the scripture (Psalm 115:17) the dead do not praise God, nor any who go down in silence. The dead do not produce eternal praise but only the contrary, eternal silence. "The living, the living man, he shall praise You" (Isaiah 38:19, NKJV).

To offer praise to God is evidence of life. It means I can feel, I can see, I can hear, and I can speak. It's the indicator that I can reason and think, and come to the conclusion that God is real and at work in my life.

It is also evidence of God's goodness toward me, which proves His worthiness of *Eternal Praise*. The mere fact that He has given life and the ability to feel, see, hear, speak, and think, gives me reason to reciprocate with a heart of thanksgiving and praise.

Some people, rather than raise their hands in praise to God, will put their hands to use with their cell phones or touching the person next to them to strike up a conversation. Others, because of pride, would rather frown and criticize those who bless God, rather than embarrass themselves by becoming clamorously foolish before the Lord. They religiously reserve their emotions and feelings for special people they love, and hold back their expressions for more meaningful moments like football games, parties, and special seasons in life. The saddest part of it all is they believe they are still alive.

Perhaps you've seen the movies that portray the individual who gets run over by a truck and walks away unscratched. They walk around through half of the movie before they realize they are actually dead. We would be shocked to know that we have people like that in the church. Dead men and women walking, those who don't eat, sleep, or reproduce as living people do. Spiritually speaking, they do not feast on the word of God, and they don't rest in the presence of the Lord, and they don't produce eternal praises for God.

The next time you are in worship service, and sit next to the person who refuses to open their mouth, or raise their hands in praise, just whisper to them politely, "remember, the dead don't praise God." When the room is filled with the exciting presence of God yet people sit with dead irresponsive blank stares on their faces, shout to the Lord, "oh Lord God, because I am alive, I will praise You." Whatever you do, don't be drawn into that dead, lethargic attitude.

Death represents the end of life. Eternal has no end. Anything dead will never produce an *Eternal Praise*. I see it too often; people come to church and offer God a dead lifeless praise. They offer words that fall from their lips to the floor. They sing songs that have no meaning to them, and play music without heart-filled worship. Because they are dead to the life in Christ Jesus, they offer praise that never reaches heaven's ears or eyes.

Another thing to note is that your praise can serve as a thermometer to gage your spiritual health, and is a remedy for your bad spiritual health. Your praise can be the medicine needed to regain spiritual vigor. It is true that when a believer does not engage in praise, something is wrong with the spirit of that person. It could be physical, emotional, or even financial, but there is something that weighs on the spirit of that individual.

The antidote prescribed by God is praise. He wants us to exchange our spirit of heaviness for His garment of praise (Isaiah 61:3). The last thing you want to do is not praise God when things are going wrong. Praise is the cure for our spiritual heaviness.

It's true, if you see a believer who does not praise God, they are no doubt sick, dead, or dying spiritually. I see it often as I lead worship; God's people struggling to praise the One who gives them life. My challenge, as a worship leader, is to help them realize they need to praise God in spite of their numbness to His goodness. It is imperative that we find the way to worship with a praise-God-anyhow attitude. It is what we were born to do. I wrote a song that I'd like you to listen to and sing along with called, "We Praise Your Name."

Eternal Praise

We Praise Your Name
by Curtis L. Butler

Verse 1:

We've gathered for one reason and one reason alone
To praise the name of Jehovah; the One Who sits upon the throne
With our instruments of Praise, with our voices upraised
We sing this joyful song. Come on everybody sing along

Chorus:

Oh Lord, we praise Your name
Oh Lord, we praise Your name
We bow down before You lifting up holy hands
There's no God beside You, no one can take Your place

Verse 2:

We were born for this purpose to worship the Holy One
To glorify the Father Who gave His only begotten Son
With our hands raised to the sky, we lift the name of the Most High
Now we sing this joyful song, Come on everybody sing along

Chorus:

Oh Lord we praise Your name, oh Lord we praise Your name
We bow down before You lifting up holy hands there's no God beside You, no one can take Your place
Oh Lord we praise Your name, Oh Lord we praise Your name

Tag:

Hallelujah, hallelujah, hallelujah, Lord, we praise You

Curtis Butler

Hallelujah, hallelujah, hallelujah, Lord, we praise You
Hallelujah, hallelujah, hallelujah, Lord, we praise Your name
Lord, we praise Your name, Jesus

The enemy fights overtime to keep us focused on our problems. But if we would just lift our eyes to God, and allow thanksgiving to come out our mouths, the heaviness will quickly lift, and we will overcome. Your bad situation may be the same, but most importantly you change.

We fight best when we are not sick with worry, fear, and doubt. When we are optimistic with faith, which is ignited by our praise, we consequently find Gods way out. We get it backward because we want to feel better before we praise God, but many times it just doesn't work that way. When we praise God, we actually lock arms with God, participating with Him as He works out our problems, and causes us to triumph in the middle of our crisis.

CHAPTER 7
Don't Stop Praising

David goes on to declare in that same Psalm 115 and verse 18 that the people of God will not be silent as the dead, but will forever bless the Lord.

...but we will bless the Lord from this time forth and forevermore.
(NKJV)

Notice that David's words are, "from this time," (right now) and going forward (for as long as) forever and more. That's an unending praise, that's Eternal Praise. What an audacious vow to make. The vow that each of us who have been saved by the grace of God must make.

When I was growing up, I'd often hear the elderly say, "Son if you can't say anything good, then don't say anything at all!" These words of wisdom got me through some real tough times, but I've learned also that if you can't think of anything good to say, just praise the Lord. I've learned to let blessings come out of my mouth rather than cursing, and positive words of praise opposed to complaining.

In order to do that, I had to fill my mind with the word of God, particularly the Psalms. The Psalms contain praise in every book, even though it is filled with life's good and not so good happenings. David was real, and he wrote songs about real life situations. He didn't hide behind a mask with a painted smile. He didn't pretend that every day was one joy.

He wrote praise songs about his many victories and his embarrassing experiences in life. David sinned, he cried, he suffered, he had days when he did not feel like singing and dancing. But no matter what the situation, in his psalm, he always concluded with praise unto a loving and merciful God.

We too have days when it looks and sound like we are losing and the devil is winning. Things might be bad, but never as bad as the enemy would make you think. When we praise the Lord, we take our focus off our negative situation, and we silence the enemy in our mind. It is a fact that the object of our focus is what we give power and credence to. When I focus on my worries, they are magnified; the more I focus on them, the greater they become.

The army of Israel could not see themselves victorious over the Philistines because of the great giant which stood before them. The more they looked at him, the greater he became in their eyes. The more they listened to him, the smaller they became in their own eyes. The

Philistine army, who knew the reputation of the Hebrew God (Yahweh), watched the Israelite soldiers shrink before them in size and spirit.

When little David showed up, he began by silencing the giant with praise to God. He spoke up with a loud voice and all the Philistines heard him. Our praise is our opinion of God concerning our situation. In 1 Samuel 17:37, David recited his opinion of the situation. He didn't allow the opinion of the giant to influence his opinion of God. Instead, he spoke words filled with faith. Our faith reveals our truest opinion of God. David's opinion was this…"The Lord Who delivered me from the paw of the lion and from the paw of the bear, He will deliver me from the hand of this Philistine." (1 Samuel 17:37, NKJV)

He said, the Lord will deliver me. Immediately David gives credit to God for His delivering power. He acknowledges God as unchangeable, because He delivered David before and is still a great Deliverer on that day. Everyone heard what the Philistine giant could do, but no one was saying what God could do, except for David. Soon David stood before his giant and recited his opinion of God in that situation.

"Then David said to the Philistine, 'You come to me with a sword, with a spear, and with a javelin, but I come to you in the name of the Lord of hosts, the God of the armies of Israel, Whom you have defied. This day the Lord will deliver you into my hand, and I will strike you and take your head from you, and this day I will give the carcasses of the camp of the Philistines to the birds of the air, and the wild beasts of the earth, that all the earth may know that there is a God in Israel.' Then all this assembly shall know that the Lord does not save with sword and spear; for the battle is the Lord's, and He will give you into our hands." (1 Samuel 17:45-47, NKJV)

Notice that David did not praise God with a song and dance, but with the fruit of his lips. He declared the Lord's name was greater than the giant's sword, spear, and javelin. David also understood that God did not need their spears and swords to deliver His children, nor did God need them to defeat the giant and the Philistine army. The more David magnified the Lord with his words, the more confident he became. His words of praise turned into faith for the Israelite army, and struck fear in the hearts of the Philistine army.

Look at the audacity of this young man as he stands flat footed with sky rocketing faith. In a sure act of bold defiance David determines to bring glory to God. We too must see any obstacle in our way as a giant who defies God. The enemy does not want God to be glorified, so we must magnify our God till He becomes bigger than our giant, and greater than our enemy's army.

We magnify God by praising Him. When God is enlarged with our words, our hearts are consumed with faith, and our actions become radical. When the enemy says you are too sick to praise God, realize that it is just his opinion. Begin to express your opinion, that God is your Healer and therefore, He is worthy of your praise. Your giant might be that you are tired from the night before, or tragedy has struck your life or a loved one, but find a way to do what David did, and kill your enemy with your praise. I'm reminded of Psalm 149:6: "Let the high praises of God be in their mouth, and a two-edged sword in their hand…"

The Scriptures go on to say that we execute vengeance against the enemy of God as we praise (Psalm 149:7-8 NKJV). This is the vengeance written against our enemy. It is with the high praises, coupled with the word of God (two-edged sword) that we bind the enemy. So rise up above your sickness, above your situation, and give your Healer the praise that He deserves.

The enemy comes to church to accuse and condemn you in the presence of God. He wants you to believe that you've sinned too much to join the congregation in praise. He will remind you that you didn't pray every day that week, or that you lied on your application and you watched the wrong TV show last night. But you must remember that there is no condemnation for those who are in Christ Jesus, who walk not after the flesh but after the Spirit (Romans 8:1). Then you must press the mute button on the accuser of the brethren (Satan). Silence him with your praise!

When we begin to praise, we not only silence the enemy but we disarm him, and our song and dance become mighty weapons. I wrote a praise song that speaks of this weapon, sing it with me:

Curtis Butler

Praise Is a Weapon
by Curtis L. Butler

Chorus:

Our praise is a weapon, proclaim it to the nations
We bind the enemy, principalities, every time we lift up a praise.
Our praise is a weapon; yes it's our declaration,
Come on and clap your hands, everybody dance,
Sing until the walls fall down.

Verse:

In our mouth is the high praises of God.
In our hands we have the two-edged sword.
We execute the vengeance of our Lord
When we praise Him, when we praise Him!

Tag:

When we praise, when we praise Him;
When we praise, the walls fall down.

We silence our enemy's accusations, his lies, and his threats when we begin to praise. Yes when we praise God we fill the atmosphere with positive proclamations of praise, leaving no space for the negative voice of the devil. Our praise should be filled with our overwhelming opinion of God, and what He says about our situation. This kind of praise comes from true revelation of God, and confidence in His great sovereignty.

Sometimes we forget who God is, and consequently we sing, we dance and play our instruments, while at the same time, having the propensity to shut off our praise whenever it inconveniences us. Sometimes we get tired, we get disconnected from the purpose of praise, and slowly the well that springs up into everlasting praise becomes a water faucet that we turn on and off.

I've had the privilege of leading worship in different denominations, and from different sides of the tracks, and we are all the same. People sing and shout their hearts out till the benediction (the closing blessing). As soon as the people of God receive their blessing, the praise is over. Let's adapt David's mentality in regard to our praise. Let's involve our will. David said, "I will bless the Lord at all times; His praise shall continually be in my mouth." (Psalm 34:1, NKJV). In the next chapter I will share my testimony of how the enemy tested this scripture in my own life.

CHAPTER 8
My Testimony

There comes a time when your belief system is put to the test. This is my testing which becomes my testimony. This concept of continual praise brings to remembrance a time of testing for me concerning this particular verse of Scripture. I wrote a song that came from Psalm 34:1, and made it my life's scripture.

I was reading and meditating on this passage of Scripture when suddenly it became revelatory to me. These words leaped into my heart, and became my personal commitment for life. Little did I know that my life's scripture would be tested. The music and words to this song just flowed out of me and onto the pages like running water. I didn't record the song for a long time, but I did teach it and used it in worship services. Finally the day came when God allowed Satan to test His Word in me.

I was sitting in my car, stranded on the side of Interstate 30 in the sweltering heat of more than 90 degrees. I patiently waited for my friend Carolyn, who was, at that time, my music secretary. I called her to see if she could pick me up. My wife Laura was away with our children at a youth camp. They took our family van because it was our best vehicle, which left me with the used car that we had just bought for my oldest son.

It was having problems with the battery going dead and needed a boost each time we drove it. We used all our extra funds for the youth camp trip, so I didn't have the money to get the car fixed yet. Nevertheless, it got me back and forth, so I intended to use it until my family returned from camp. There I was, home alone with just a few responsibilities to handle.

One of those responsibilities was praise practice on Saturday. We lived in Dallas and our church was in Ft. Worth, which was about an hour's drive away. I have always found it difficult to cancel a practice, so in spite of my malfunctioning vehicle, I was determined to not only make rehearsal on Saturday, but Sunday service as well.

I had this new song that God had given me that I felt strongly about teaching the praise team for our congregation. I loaded up my keyboard, my amplifier, my music for practice, and, saying a quick prayer, cranked up the car and headed for praise practice. Practice was awesome! The Spirit of God was present as we sang my new song. The name of the song was "Bless the Lord." This song was an inspiration from Psalm 34:1, where David said "I will bless the Lord at all times; His praise shall continually be in my mouth."

Eternal Praise

Let's take a quick praise break, sing this song with me.

Bless the Lord
by Curtis L. Butler

Verse 1:

Trials come, but they will never stop my song
I will praise Your name on high
When things go right, when things go wrong
I'll lift my praise to the sky

Chorus:

Bless the Lord at all times, Bless the Lord at all times
Bless the Lord at all times, Bless the Lord at all times

Verse 2:

We offer up the sacrifice of praise
Unto God continually, (yeah)
The fruit of our lips will give Him praise
And His wonderful acts we will proclaim

Chorus:

Bless the Lord at all times, Bless the Lord at all times
Bless the Lord at all times, Bless the Lord at all times

Bridge:

And His praise shall continually be in my mouth
Yes His praise shall continually be in my mouth
Oh His praise shall continually be in my mouth
Yes His praise shall continually be in my mouth

I will bless the Lord

Tag:

Bless the Lord oh my soul and all that is within me
I will, I will bless the Lord at all times
I will bless the Lord

After practice, the car started up and I was on my way home, singing my new song, and having visions of what the next day's service was going to be like. The next thing I know I was watching cars and trucks zoom past me on the Interstate as I sat in my car, which refused to go any further.

If it had been a flat tire, I could have easily fixed it and been on my way laughing at the devil; however, it turned out to be the alternator, for which I had no money to repair. One minute I was in the presence of the heavenly host as we sang "Bless the Lord at All Times," and 30 minutes later, I found myself alienated from everyone, even God. I called my dear sister in the Lord, Carolyn, and she said she'd be right out to get me.

After a few minutes of waiting, I felt a strong desire to complain to God. I could have cancelled praise practice and made arrangements for someone to pick me up for Sunday morning service, but I felt compelled to take my chances with the car and trust God to get me through it. Some people might call it foolishness, others might call it faith, but as my father-in law would say, in his rough and raspy voice, "God takes care of fools and babes." I suppose I was both in this situation.

Eternal Praise

As you can guess, the devil began to whisper in the ears of my soulish man; "I can understand this whole thing happening if you had been trying to go to a movie or some place you should not go, but you were trying to act on faith and do the work of God. How could this have happened to you?"

Suddenly it hit me like an S.K.U.D. missile that my faith in the words of my song was being tested. The question was not how could this have happened to me? The question was, would I really bless the Lord at all times? Could my situation be an exception to the rule? Do I need to rethink the scripture and rewrite the song? Does the phrase "at all times" really mean ALL times? Then I heard myself laugh, as I began to sing rather than complain.

I was still stranded, but I was not abandoned, because help was on the way. I was still out there by myself, but I was not alone as I felt the angelic host gather around me while I sang. Instead of feeling like God was doing nothing about my situation, I felt like all of heaven was dispatched on my behalf, and God was doing something big for me.

When Carolyn arrived, she insisted that I let her take me all the way to my house, which was 25 or 30 miles out of her way. I thanked her, and I thanked the Lord for His goodness toward me. About an hour later I received a call from Carolyn's husband, Walter. He informed me that they were on their way to my house with one of their cars for me to use to get to church on Sunday morning. I was so overwhelmed that I again began to bless the Lord. When Walter and Carolyn arrived, I apologized that I didn't have money to compensate them for the gas they had used on my behalf. Walter would not hear of it, he just handed me the keys and assured me there was plenty gas in the car for me to use it as I needed. Walter then gave me one of those big bear hugs that only he could give, and they left me there in tears of gratitude. I felt like a real King's kid.

My wife called that night and I told her what had happened and we blessed the Lord some more. The next day I went to church praising God the whole way, and we blessed the Lord as a congregation. After church service, I was approached by another brother, named Michael, like the Archangel. He offered to fix my car free of charge, and all I needed to do was buy the part. Then my pastor, Patrick McGrew, Sr. offered to buy the part and take me out to dinner. Needless to say, my cup was running over. There I was with a fixed car, full stomach, and heart bubbling over with joy. I believe that it was because I chose to bless the Lord when I had every reason to do otherwise.

These words, "bless the Lord at all times," have been the chorus or the hook in many praise and worship songs today, but until we grasp the full meaning of them, they are just words of an overzealous psalmist. When David said, "I will bless the Lord," he had thought it out, came to a resolve, and made a choice. He understood that times and seasons will change, which tend to dictate our behaviors and our attitudes. He knew there might be times when he would not be able to muster up the strength to raise up a praise, but would have to somehow keep his vow to bless the Lord God at all times.

We too must come to resolve that though it may not be easy, we will bless God as David did while running from King Saul. Find a way to not complain, as suffering Job did, when we don't understand why.

Even as the Apostle Paul did, as he fought the good fight of faith, and as Jesus did from birth to burial. Let's make it our life's goal to give God a praise that never quits; an Eternal Praise.

CHAPTER 9
Eternality of Words

Usually when we praise, whether audibly or written, we use words. So let's look closer at the spiritual side of our words. First, we must understand that words are eternal, and once they are spoken they exist as sound waves in the atmosphere forever. Waves are invisible to the natural eye, and the invisible is eternal. 2 Corinthians 4:18 says, "While we do not look at the things which are seen, but at the things which are not seen. For the things which are seen are temporary, but the things which are not seen are eternal." (NKJV)

In this passage of scripture, the apostle Paul is making a comparison between two opposites, the natural body and the spiritual body; the perishing outward man and the renewed inward man, the seen and the unseen. But the principle can easily be applied to my point because words too are invisible, and unseen, but once they are spoken they are eternal.

It is a proven fact that if we had a microphone powerful enough, we could actually hear the Gettysburg Address, the "I Have a Dream" speech of Dr. Martin Luther King Jr., even the first words recorded in scripture by God Himself, "Let there be…" These words and others today are still reverberating in outer space. We must understand that words are eternal and when they are spoken they materialize over time, especially if we water them with our actions. That is why we should be careful what words come forth from our mouth (Proverbs 18:21; Matthew 12:37).

The only appropriate praise for an eternal God is Eternal Praise. As I've already stated, praise is simply the act of expressing a good opinion of something or someone. According to scriptural examples of praise, we should praise God with…

Yadah (yaw-daw', H3034, Strong's Hebrew Lexicon), to show reverence or praise with extended hands.

Towdah, (to-daw', H8426, Strong's Hebrew Lexicon), to show agreement with the extending of the right hand or thankfulness.

Barak (baw-rak', H1288, Strong's Hebrew Lexicon): to kneel down, or bow low in adoration.

Hallal (haw-lal', H1984, Strong's Hebrew Lexicon): to be clamorously foolish, to boast and shine, to celebrate.

Shabach, (shaw-bakh', H7623, Strong's Hebrew Lexicon): to address in a loud tone, to shout.

Tehillah (te-hil-law', H8416, Strong's Hebrew Lexicon) to sing spontaneously to the Lord, a new song.

Zamar (zaw-mar', H2167, Strong's Hebrew Lexicon): to pluck the strings, to celebrate in song and music or just music.

These are all outward acts of praise and are quite appropriate when using all that God requires of us in praise. However the most common way we praise is with the fruit of our lips. If we are not musically inclined, if we are physically handicapped, if we don't have a demonstrative personality, we can yet praise God with our words.

Words are not only eternal in nature, like God, but they also possess God-given power. It was with His words that God created all living things. God's word, even today, echos throughout time and eternity. As a result, things are being created and recreated every second.

Sometimes our words are like weeds, because once we have spoken them, they quickly take root and grow, sometimes they grow even if we don't water them. They grow in the most unusual places in our lives. I've seen weeds that grew from under a concrete sidewalk, breaking through the hard substance and the smallest cracks. They can grow under heavy rocks and tall buildings. Weeds can grow in the driest climates, as well as in tropical places. The best way to rid them is to pull them up from the root, and still you might catch them coming back later. Our words can be like weeds, because once they are spoken they are almost certain to manifest somewhere, somehow, at some time.

I've heard it said, "Sticks and stones may break my bones, but words will never hurt me." My life experiences have proven differently. I am still in recovery from some of the words that were spoken to, and over, me as a child. In some ways, I walk through life with a limp because of hurtful words that were spoken over me. However, there have been some positive words spoken over me as well; words that became the cane I needed to keep me going forward, in spite of my limp.

I easily recall those prophetic words that were spoken over me in my past, and I have seen them amazingly manifest in my present day. For instance, a powerful woman of God spoke to me and said that I would lead thousands upon thousands in worship to God; that I would play my piano and sing on a platform before multitudes of people. As a teenager living in a small town, and just learning to play the piano at that time, this was way bigger than I could wrap my brain around. Nonetheless, I chose to believe and receive her prophetic words, and then I just left it all in God's hands. Years later I found myself standing on a stage before thousands leading them in worship just as that woman had spoken.

Even before that, I recall my mother speaking to me as a child. I had been underweight, short, and timid all my life, but my mom (Idell, what a beautiful name) took my little hands into hers and said many times to me, "God has given you big hands, and that means you will do big things in life." Over the years, the size of my hands didn't change much; in fact my hands have always been rather small. However, these small hands have created artworks that brought me before great men. These small hands have written powerful songs and now books. These small hands play melodies that have transformed countless lives, and shifted atmospheres.

Eternal Praise

Most recently God spoke through my pastor during an altar call. He called me from the piano, laid hands on me, and said God was downloading new songs into my spirit and he began to count the songs. Immediately I began to hear new music and fresh words. Even today I still receive from that prophecy as those words reverberate in my mind. This book is a product of the words Pastor Patrick McGrew, Sr. has spoken over my life. It is no small thing to me when words come my way, or proceed out of my own mouth. Our words, no matter how meaningless they seem, hold value and great significance.

There are other examples of the power of words. I recall my auntie, and other relatives, saying to my cousins, words like, "You are never going to be much." "You are just like your sorry daddy," they'd say. I would hear them laugh as they'd say things like "he's going to be a woman chaser." or "you will never keep a steady job." They took great pleasure in predicting their daughter's future when they would say, "she's going to be pregnant before she's eighteen."

The negative words, as harmless as they seemed, just went on and on and on. Sure enough, my cousin turned out to be exactly like his daddy, he was a woman chaser, and couldn't keep a steady job. His sister got pregnant as a teen, and lived on welfare for most of her life. This crazy cycle continued as the children grew up to be parents and repeated their parent's erroneous ways. They spoke negative things over their own children. These stories are more common than we'd like to think. The invisible words we speak, whether positive or negative, will manifest over time, unless we change what we say.

When we understand and acknowledge the potency of our words, we can appreciate their significance in our praise. What we say about God and about our situations matter. We should purpose in our hearts to bless, and not curse, with our words. Possessing the power to speak life or death, positive or negative, good or bad, is one of the Godly traits given to us by our Creator God (Proverbs 18:21; Matthew 12:37). We have been trusted with the responsibility to use this Godly trait to bless, specifically to bless the Lord. Again David said in Psalm 34:1,

"I will bless the Lord at all times and His praise shall continually be in my mouth."

Think about this, if blessings are in our mouth all the time, then we have no time or energy for cursing and negative murmuring. We must purposefully use our words for the most positive effect. Let's sing these words to a song that the Holy Spirit inspired me to write about our God.

Eternal Praise

My Everything

by Curtis L. Butler

Lord, You are my love
Lord, You are my joy
Lord, You are my peace within
King of Kings, You are my everything
Lord, You are my hope
Lord, You are my song
Lord, You are my power and strength
King of kings, You are my everything
You are my everything, everything
King of kings, You're my everything

My everything, Lord, You are everything to me
The air I breath, the song I sing
The very life that flows through my vein
My everything, Alpha Omega Beginning and End
My aspirations, my dreams, my past
My future, and everything between
I'm overwhelmed, as it's plain to see, Lord
You are my everything.

Lord, You are my night, when the sun goes down
Lord, You are my day, and when it comes back around
Lord, You are the Light of my life
King of kings, You are my everything.

CHAPTER 10
Eternality Of Music

Often our words of praise are transported by our music into the atmosphere, engulfing all who are near. Music softens hearts, open minds, and invites the listener to think and embrace our words. Music is also eternal; it too is invisible like our audible words, and has no end. Music is like God in that we can't see it but we see the evidence of its reality. We can't reach out and hold the sounds, but we can feel them, and this very much affects our behavior, our mood, and emotions.

I've learned that music has an undeniable effect on the human being. Not just the physical part of us, but also the spirit and soul. We should be aware that every man is made up of three distinct parts. We are body, spirit and soul. Our body is the physical, earthly part of us that we can see. We often think it is the real us because it is the part we discover first in life.

Shortly afterwards, we understand there is another part called the soul. The soul is one of the invisible parts of man encompassing the mind, will, emotions, and intellect of an individual. We struggle with the soul-ish part of us, and work hard at catering to it.

Finally, as we begin to search deeper, we unveil the spirit. The spirit of the individual is the part that is most like God. The Bible says in John 4:24 that God is Spirit. Our spirit is the inner part of us, the other invisible part. It is the part that is eternal like God and houses the soul (which Jesus died to save). One of the things that make these three entities one is that they are all affected by music.

Not many realize that music enhances brain development, and is a form of psychotherapy. In the 17th century, the scholar, Robert Burton's The Anatomy of Melancholy argued that music and dance are critical in treating mental illness. The word "music" is derived from the Greek word mousike, which means "art of the muses," and muses were a group of Greek goddesses that promoted literature and the arts. The word "muse" actually means to learn or to think. So music would be a progressive combination of organized sounds that causes one to learn or to think.

How we feel at any given time can easily be traced back to the music we habitually listen to. Scientists say that classical music, which is produced mostly by stringed instruments, makes better thinkers. String music, when played in a certain manner, soothes and calms us down. We must also note the loud guitars, also stringed instruments, when played by the rock musician, will open our souls to whatever lyrics are being screamed. Consequently, what happens is that music opens your mind, and subconsciously, the words go deep, till you begin to muse or think about the words that you hear.

As a visual artist, I tend to be more creative when the strings are being played. So I will sometimes play classical music, which is mostly stringed instruments of an orchestra, to help me relax and think out of the box.

Music also makes work go faster and smoother. While we are being amused by our favorite style of music, we tend to lose track of time. In a sense, we actually step out of time and into eternity where time does not exist. Music has a history of helping us get through the toughest times, as it did for many African Americans who lived during the days of slavery in America. It was the music of Blacks in America that strengthened their faith, gave them hope, and encouraged them as they suffered extreme prejudice and injustice.

There was good news found in songs like By and By, Goin' Up Yonder, and I'll Fly Away. And those who did not go to church found strength in singing the blues, which allowed them to let out their frustrations, cry their tears, and moan in a soulful rhythmic way. Little did we know that the same scientific proof that I share with you in this book was working for us as we listened and sang those songs. The anesthetic effect of music has provided many people, not just Blacks, the strength to overcome the most horrific tragedies of life.

Millions of dollars are spent strategically everyday on researching and creating the right music to be played in shopping malls. The strategy is to help shoppers relax and stay around to spend more money.

Music has been used to create a sense of reality within the sub-consciousness of people for centuries.

Hollywood discovered this early on as the movie industry evolved to the mega billion dollar business that it is today. It all started with silent motion pictures, which had no sound. They were entertaining, but people wanted more. Words were added to the visuals as captions for the viewer to read along with the movie. Then sound was added, which was revolutionary. It made what was seen on the screen come to life, engaging the eyes and ears and the brains of the viewers. It is the music in the background that gives the feelings of suspense, terror, romance, comedy, sorrow, or joy.

Music is also hypnotic in that it kept the viewer involved and connected to the story. People would be so engrossed in the movie that their minds would forget present realities around them, and be transported to wherever the movie took them. This gives great power to the possessor. The ones who had ability to produce music possessed significant influence over any listener. Those of us who play instruments, or produce musical pieces, need to be aware of our influence. We should study to be knowledgeable and careful how we then use this notable power.

Eternal Praise

Everything That Has Breath
by Curtis L. Butler

Everything that has breath praise the Lord
Everything that has breath praise the Lord
Praise Him in the sanctuary
Praise Him in His might and in His power
Praise Him for His mighty deeds
According to His excellent greatness
Everybody ought to praise Him

Everything that has breath praise the Lord
Everything that has breath praise the Lord

Praise Him with sound of the trumpet
On the harp and the stringed instruments
Praise Him with the tambourine and the dance
With stringed instruments and organs
With all kinds of blessings
Bless His Name!

Everything that has breath praise the Lord
Everything that has breath praise the Lord

Let all creation in heaven and all the earth
Declare His glory, hallelujah, Praise the Lord

Praise the Lord! I'm sure as you listened to the instruments in this song that you felt its power come over you to respond. I hope you took that time to do more than listen, but to praise the Lord. My study has proven that music comes from God, the Creator of every good and perfect gift (James 1:17). Music is important to God, and it played a part in His creative work in the beginning. In the book of Job, we see where musical sounds filled the atmosphere while God created. Let's read... Job 38:1-7

> *Then the Lord spoke to Job out of the storm. He said: 'Who is this that obscures My plans with words without knowledge? Brace yourself like a man; I will question you, and you shall answer Me. Where were you when I laid the foundation? Tell me if you understand. Who marked off its dimensions? Surely you know! Who stretched a measuring line across it? On what were its footings set, or Who laid its cornerstone; while the morning stars sang together, and all the angels shouted for joy?' (NIV)*

In this passage of Scripture, we would normally focus on the main characters, God and Job. Job has just laid before God some questions. God reciprocates with His own set of questions. In the process of questioning Job, God discloses some interesting information. There was singing going on during the creative work of God. While God was busy laying the foundations, marking off its dimensions, measuring it all out, setting the footings, and laying the cornerstone of all creation, the morning stars sang together and the angels shouted.

Eternal Praise

The morning stars are thought to have been Jesus the "Bright and Morning Star" (Revelation 22:16) and Lucifer, who is also known as the "Star of the Morning" (Isaiah 14:12, NASB). Lucifer is recorded as having instruments built into his body (Ezekiel 28:13), so there could have been instrumental music as well. The angels shouted, which sounds a lot like our church service. Perhaps the Morning Stars sang the words of God as He saw His creation and declared it good, and the angels shouted "amen!" in agreement with God. Maybe they sang hallelujahs as they all celebrated the awesomeness of God's creative genius. We don't know, but we can safely speculate from these passages of scripture that singing, shouting, and possibly instrumental music was present at creation.

God loves music so much that He created the perfect musician for heaven's worship, as I previously mentioned. In heaven, God had three Archangels; Michael the warrior angel, Gabriel the messenger angel, and Lucifer the worshipping angel. Each of these three ruling angels commanded a third of heaven's angels, each as service to God.

There are many scriptures that reveal each angel performing his own assigned duties. Careful study of scripture reveals interesting facts about Lucifer, now known as Satan. One of Lucifer's responsibilities was to lead the heavens in worship unto God. Scripture tells us that Lucifer's body was created with the three families of instruments built inside of him. Yes the wind, the strings, and the percussion instruments were built into Lucifer's body. God was strategic and specific about Lucifer's make up, so that he could fulfill his purpose in heaven.

Ezekiel 28:13 says, "Thou hast been in Eden the garden of God; every precious stone was thy covering, the sardius, topaz, and the diamond, the beryl, the onyx, and the jasper, the sapphire, the emerald, and the carbuncle, and gold: the workmanship of thy tabrets (percussion instrument) and of thy pipes (the wind instrument) was prepared in thee in the day that thou wast created." (KJV) (parenthetics mine)

Earlier in Isaiah 14:11-12 we see that Lucifer's body also had stringed instruments built in. "Thy pomp is brought down to the grave, the noise of thy viols (from where we get our word violin): the worm is spread under thee and the worms cover thee. How art thou fallen from heaven O Lucifer, son of the morning! How art thou cut down to the ground, which didst weaken the nations!" (KJV) (parenthetics mine)

Tabrets, pipes and viols, these are the instruments named as part of Lucifer's body. He did not have to pick up a violin because he had viols in his body. Lucifer did not have to find a drum-set to play because he was the tambourine. Because Lucifer had pipes built in his body he needed no trumpet, flute or pipe organ. And here in scripture, Lucifer, as one of the morning stars, apparently sang.

Jesus is also known as the Bright and Morning Star. He sang in heaven as indicated in Job 38:1-7, and He sang on earth with His disciples at the last supper. We must remember that Jesus was a Jew and practiced traditional Jewish customs. God's people sang and danced a lot, and enjoyed it. God sings over us with rejoicing according to Zephaniah 3:17. Music and singing started with God in creation, and it ends with God in Revelation. God loves, and uses music. I believe it is God's desire that we use music to bring glorious praise to Him.

We, as musicians and singers, must understand and use, with extreme caution, the gifts God has given us. We can use music for many things, in many ways, but I'm convinced that the one main purpose for music, musical instruments, and musicians is to first bring honor and glory to God. Many musicians have used music for personal enjoyment, others as a means of gaining wealth. I'm not implying that those things are wrong, but I say that, if we are not glorifying the Giver with the gift given, we are not fulfilling the true purpose of our gift.

Myles Monroe said, "Where purpose is not known, abuse is inevitable." He goes on to make his point by saying "You may take a microphone and use it as a drumstick, it will make a beautiful sound, but a microphone is not created for that purpose. As a drumstick, we never hear its most beautiful sound until we use it the way it was originally intended. Its true purpose is found in the mind of the creator." (Azusa Conference, Tulsa OK).

If you are a musician of any genre of music I implore you to make the connection with the Giver of your gift, and find out for what purpose you were entrusted with it. With that revelation, you will find greater fulfillment in the music you play, thereby bringing glory to God.

The inventor of the microphone intended for it to be used to amplify the voice. To use it otherwise would be abuse, or abnormal. There are notable musicians who make music strictly for the goal of obtaining wealth, glory, and fame. Consequently we get music that does not glorify God, but instead, brings Him shame. If these things are our goals, then we are willing to produce any type of music, even if that means demeaning women, encouraging violence and hate, or cursing the Giver of gifts. Don't stop with this book, but go on to do more study on your own, and seek out the true purpose of the gift of music. With these instruments, we create an atmosphere for God to meet with His people.

In my personal study, I've found that music affects the three entities of man. The spirit, soul, and body of man is spiritually and physically connected to music. The string instruments affect the soul, which houses the mind, the will, the intellect, and the emotions of man.

The wind instruments effect the spirit of man, as does the blast of the trumpets used to sound an alarm. They affect the inner heart, the real you. For example, the blast of the ram's horn or trumpet arouses the spirit of the soldiers. The trumpets are also played to alarm people or call them together, and to battle. Marching bands use mostly instruments of the brass or wind family. The wind instrument's sound not only can fill vast amounts of open outdoor space, but also arouses the inner man to rise up and react.

The percussion instrument affects the physical body of man. It is scientifically proven that man has an innate desire to be in sync; meaning that, when we hear a steady beat, we naturally want to become one with it. It is the beat of a song that makes our very heart beat faster or slower. Marching bands are mostly composed of the wind instruments because the piercing sound they make can fill the vast open atmosphere with excitement. At the sound of the trumpet, the dead in Christ shall rise (1 Thessalonians 4:16).

The wind is also synonymous with the Holy Spirit of God. In Acts 2:2-4 the Spirit of God is said to have come like the sound of a mighty rushing wind." Our spirit, the inner man, is sometimes referred to as the heart or core of our being. Study teaches that our spirit houses the soul, which is the mind, will, emotions and intellect of a person. The spirit of man is the invisible part of us and it is that part of us that is most like God, because "God is a Spirit" (1 Corinthians 6:17). Remember Scripture says, "God is a Spirit and they that worship Him must worship Him in spirit and in truth. (John 4:24, KJV)

I learned that the percussion instruments move the physical body of a man. As mentioned earlier, when we hear a steady rhythm or feel a strong beat, we innately desire to get in sync with it. I don't know anyone who can listen to a beat and not want to tap their feet, bounce their head, or move their body to its rhythm. God has so created us that we naturally respond to the repetitious beat. This is a beautiful reality.

Let's do a self-test; play some music with a strong beat, sit, relax, and listen to the rhythm of the beat. See if you can sit still for very long. If you can do it without moving to the beat, it's because you are trying very hard not to be moved. When music and words are combined, we have a powerful weapon that can be used to influence people. I often use this knowledge to enhance our worship services. I've learned that certain chords and progressions create specific atmospheres and that different sounds inspire the people deep within their spirit, soul, and their body.

CHAPTER 11
Eternal Warfare

Allow me to now take a portion of this book to look at praise as a warrior's weapon, King David saw it. In Psalm 149 verses 6-9 the Psalmist writes these words,

May the praise of God be in their mouths and a double-edged sword in their hands, to inflict vengeance on the nations and punishment on the peoples, to bind their kings with fetters, their nobles with shackles of iron, to carry out the sentence written against them, this is the glory of all His faithful people. Praise the Lord. (NIV)

Note that the writer is exhorting us, the people of God, to praise the Lord. The passage starts out with "Praise the Lord" (vs 1) and then ends with "Praise the Lord." The books that precede it are about praising the Lord and the last Book of Psalm (Psalm 150) again encourages everything that has breath to praise the Lord. All of a sudden in the same breath the writer equates praise with warfare. To the psalmist, praise and warfare are the same. Could it be that our praise then is a spiritual weapon?

Let's step out of time for a moment into the eternal place and discover how this eternal warfare began. I've shared already with you about Lucifer, the anointed cherub. He was created by God in perfection. Lucifer was attributed the responsibility of leading the heavens in worship unto God.

The Bible declares that Lucifer was beautiful and his body was covered with all kinds of precious stones. Lucifer also covered the Throne of God. Which means that The Light of God (Scripture bears out that God is light) beaming through the multicolored stones of Lucifer's body probably exuded beautiful rays of glorious light in the heavens. Earlier, I shared how Lucifer's body makeup consisted of the three families of instruments. Lucifer possessed the wind (pipes), the percussion (tabrets also known as the tambourine) and the strings family (viols where we get the word violin and viola). With these instruments, he created beautiful sounds for worship unto God. Lucifer was gifted to do so many things with excellence. The Bible says Lucifer was perfect until iniquity was found in him (Ezekiel 28:15). The iniquity found in him was the sin of pride, which led to rebellion against God. Lucifer was then cast down to earth where he became known as the devil, Satan, and the serpent (Revelation 12:9).

Lucifer lost that battle for God's throne, but is determined not to lose the war for worship. He desires to have a throne of his own to be worshipped above God. Satan desires the Eternal Praise. This praise was only meant for our eternal God. So Satan does everything in his power and wit to distract us from worshipping God and to consequently begin worshipping him. Deep inside of Satan there exists a burning desire to be worshipped as God, which he will never get unless he is able to first silence our praises to God.

We are busy fighting, biting, and devouring one another, while our real enemy is laughing and watching us self-destruct. The Bible says we wrestle not against flesh and blood, but principalities and spiritual wickedness in high places (Ephesians 6:12). I realize that my brother or sister is not my enemy, and that my battle is not against those I can see, but that which I cannot see. It is against the evil spirits that influence them to do wickedness against me. When I retaliate, I must make sure to love the offending person, while I aim my weapon at the spirit around them. So when I read Psalm 149 (as well as many other passages that refer to wars and fighting in the Bible) I connect, through the discernment of the Holy Spirit, with what the writer is saying about nations, peoples, kings and nobles. For me, this Scripture is speaking of the devil and his kingdom of demonic spirits. I see the prophetic message behind it.

We know that in the book of Deuteronomy the Canaanites, and the surrounding nations, occupied the promised land of the Children of Israel. They were real people, and a physical enemy of God and the Children of Israel. They were worshippers of Baal (the most worshipped god of the Canaanites) and Asherah (The Canaanite, mother-goddess of the sea, a female consort of Baal). Those who worshipped these gods practiced idolatry and immorality.

God judged them for their sins, and sentenced them to be defeated by the Israelites and totally destroyed. God's reason for this was three-fold; first, it was to judge the people of that land for their sins. Secondly, to fulfill God's promise to Moses and the Children of Israel, and thirdly, to protect God's chosen people from being drawn away from God's favor, and ruined by the idolatry and immorality of those nations.

When I read the Scriptures from a New Testament believer's point of view, it is easy to identify my real enemy. The reality is that I am not living in that day and time, and those people do not hold my promise. Nor do these nations hold a threat to my right relationship with God. It would be evident that the nations and government spoken of in Psalm 149 is spiritual, not physical. The weapons that I use must also then be spiritual. Our weapons are our high praises of God and the two-edged sword (His Word). These are the weapons chosen by God for the praiser to use in executing vengeance and carrying out the sentence written against our enemy. Who is our enemy? The accuser of the brethren, Satan and his spiritual army, is our enemy.

Again, he is a spiritual enemy, so our weapons must be spiritual. Our weapons are not carnal but mighty through God to the pulling down of strong-holds (2 Corinthians 10:4). In Hebrews 4:12 the word of God is compared to a two-edged sword. It says,

For the Word of God is alive and active. Sharper than a double edged sword, it penetrates even to the dividing of soul and spirit, joints and marrow; it judges the thoughts and attitude of the heart.

(NIV)

We saw where the Scripture says we are to arrest and drive out nations and people, bind kings and nobles with fetters and iron shackles. We are to execute vengeance, and to carry out the sentence that is written against the enemy of God. It goes on to say this is the glory of all His people. We are His people, the sheep of His pasture and therefore we have this glorious privilege.

Let's rise up and do battle against the enemy of our souls. The Scripture makes it clear that Satan has come to kill, steal, and destroy (John 10:10). When Jesus came, He overcame the devil, death, hell, and the grave (Colossians 2:15). He now holds all power of heaven and earth in His hands (Matthew 28:18). You might say that our fight is fixed because we war against an already defeated foe. All that is left is for us is to praise God and declare His Word in times of battle.

I'm reminded of a passage of Scripture when the man of God sent out the praisers first and brought forth victory. 2 Chronicles 20:20-24 reads,

Early in the morning they left for the desert of Tekoa. As they set out, Jehoshaphat stood and said, 'Listen to me, Judah and people of Jerusalem! Have faith in the Lord your God and you will be upheld; have faith in His prophets and you will be successful.' After

consulting the people, Jehoshaphat appointed men to sing to the Lord and praise Him for the splendor of His holiness as they went out at the head of the army saying: 'Give thanks to the Lord, for His love endures forever.'

As they began to sing and praise, the Lord set ambushes against the men of Amon, and Moab, and Mount Seir who were invading Judah, and they were defeated. The Ammonites and Moabites rose up against the men from Mount Seir to destroy and annihilate them. After they finished slaughtering the men from Seir, they helped destroy one another. When the men of Judah came to the place that overlooks the desert and looked toward the vast army, they saw only dead bodies lying on the ground. No one had escaped."
(NIV)

This passage of Scripture shows praise being used to defeat a physical enemy. As the singers went out in front of the Israelite army, they sang praises to the Lord God, which is a spiritual act of worship. God then set ambushes against their enemies, which is a physical act of warfare. God destroyed and annihilated the vast army till none were left alive.

When we sing praises, God is postured to defend us. Just as a father who hears his son bragging on him to his friends, God wants to prove us right in our opinion of Him and His faithfulness to us. Israel did nothing, but first praised the Lord, secondly took faith in what God told the prophets, and thirdly collected the spoils (vs. 25). And so, praise is used as a weapon of warfare, and can be used in the same way by those of us who would dare to offer praise in difficult times.

Please note that Israel praised before, during, and after the battle. This kind of praise is eternal. Think about it like this, the eternal God, (who holds our victory) is powerful before the battle begins, during the battle, and after the battle is over. Let's practice praising God continually, that is before our tests, during our time of testing, and after we pass the test. This makes our praise an Eternal Praise. Let's start now praising God with this song titled "Victory." Perhaps it will rise up in our hearts when the battle is raging, when the battle is over, and again, when you have obtained the promised victory, praise God even more. Let's not wait for the battle to begin, let's engage in warfare right now with this song of praise!

Curtis Butler

Victory

by Curtis L. Butler

Chorus:

I have victory, with my Lord and King

He has given me victory, victory. (repeat)

Verse 1:

In a world that's slowly dying

And the light has grown so dim

Winners are constantly loosing strength they once found deep down within

We must keep our eyes on Jesus, the Author and Finisher of our faith

He alone is able to assure us victory in all that we face

Chorus:

Verse 2:

The army of God is marching

And they're moving across this land

With the high praises of God on their lips

And a two-edged sword in their hands

Keeping their eyes on Jesus

The Commander and Chief in charge

He alone is able to assure us victory

As we fight this spiritual war

Chorus:

(Rock Guitar Solo)

Eternal Praise

Chant 1:

We are soldiers for the Lord
Fighting hell with all our heart
Victory is our battle cry
Busting demons left and right
Waging war on sin and shame
Stepping out in Jesus name
Some don't like it we don't care
Cause we're a witness to the world

Chant 2:

Warring in the heavenlies, overcoming principalities
Putting demons on the run, praising God for what He's done
Read God's Word, fast and pray, getting stronger everyday
Stalking sinners in the night, bringing souls into the light
V. I. C. T. O. R. Y.
(repeat it till you believe it)

CHAPTER 12
In the Spirit, In the Eternal

There he sat in solitude, totally separated from all that was familiar. He had no family, no friends, nor anything that remotely resembled home, often, sleeping in cold damp caves, sharing meager existence with the wild beasts of the island. This elderly apostle is none other than the one known as "The Beloved." He, who knew intimately the Truth, is now denied his right to the very freedom that is promised to those who know the Truth.

He was strategically placed on an abandoned piece of earth to be quietly forgotten. To be tortured and killed in the sight of the other believers would be too risky. The last thing needed was another martyr to live down. No, this was the best way to rid the contemporary society of the last of the chosen disciples.

The plot was to eradicate the effects of that fearless twelve who walked and talked with the King of the Jews. With nowhere else to go on the Lord's Day, this aged Apostle began to seek the Lord, and found a door to an eternal place, and was invited by an eternal Being to enter therein. His name was John, also known as John the Revelator. He was responsible for writing the Book of Revelation, the final of the 66 books accepted as the canon.

I've always admired John in that He really loved Jesus. It must be noted that he, John, is found nearest Jesus at the Last Supper. And before that, he was one of the three there at the transfiguration as part of Jesus' inner circle. He was nearest Jesus at the Crucifixion. John was the one that Jesus assigned the responsibility of caring for Mary, Jesus' Mother.

I'm sure after witnessing the horrible deaths of almost all of the original twelve, and seeing those who were killed, one by one, go to be with their Lord that by now, John was longing to do the same. But God, in His infinite wisdom kept death away from this gentle servant. It is when we read the book of Revelation that we see why John's life was so preserved. Yes, John's vision revealed to all of us the things that are to come. He also unveils the mysteries of heaven's worship and how we should model our worship on earth.

It is from this passage of scripture that I was inspired to write the song "Eternal Praise." John introduces the New Testament believer to eternal worship, which we can use as our worship manual, from which we want to adapt our example of true worship. Eternal worship is worship that happens within the spirit realm. The Scripture says that John was in the spirit on the Lord's Day. Let's read Revelations 1:10,

> *On the Lord's Day, I was in the Spirit. And I heard behind me a loud voice like a trumpet, which said; "Write on a scroll what you see and send it to the seven churches; to Ephesus, Smyrna, Pergamum, Thyatira, Sardis, Philadelphia, and Laodicea. (NIV)*

John says he was in the Spirit. What does it mean to be in the Spirit? The Old Testament demonstrates the Spirit of God descending on a person, resting in a place or hovering over as in Genesis. But it is in the New Testament that it becomes possible to be in the Spirit. To be in the Spirit is to be completely submerged, surrounded, and filled inside and out with the presence of the Holy Spirit of God. It is to connect your spirit with the very Spirit of God (1 Corinthians 6:17). Remember in John 4: 23-24 it says,

> *Yet a time is coming and has now come, when the true worshippers will worship the Father in the Spirit and in truth, for they are the kind of worshippers the Father seeks. God is Spirit and His worshippers must worship Him in the Spirit and in truth. (NIV)*

These are the words of Jesus, the Son of God, and He says that it is "in the Spirit and in truth" that we are to worship God. Our geographical location of worship is not as important as our spiritual location. If we are to really connect with God in our worship, we need to get in the

Spirit. It is there where we hear His voice and see what He sees. We church goers have erroneously resolved, as did the Samaritan woman, that our geographical location of worship is the most important thing.

The big question is always where do you worship? A better question is have you been worshipping in the Spirit? Far too many show up at that designated place on Sundays to perform an act of worship, by clapping, praying, singing, reading the Word of God, and even dancing. We go through the motions, but we never get in the Spirit. Consequently our worship service becomes lifeless, mundane and predictable. I know because I've been there too many times.

I believe that being in the Spirit is to be in another place, an eternal place. A place where time has no limits and does not dictate how high, how deep, or long we go. I shift from one reality to another, and I'm able to somehow tap into a sixth sense. Spiritual things become so clearly understood as I am closer to God than ever before. When I am in the Spirit, I lose track of time, and often everything around me fades, as the presence of God consumes me. My attention is on God the Father, God the Son, and God the Holy Spirit.

My time in the Spirit has many times offended others. They didn't sense the same freedom because they were ready to go on to other things deemed important on the service agenda. Don't get me wrong I've been a worship leader long enough to understand the importance of doing things decently and in order, especially when it comes to congregational worship. Part of my responsibility is to guard the flow of service, especially when I'm in charge. This means I must respect the directives prescribed in order to accomplish the set goals and objectives for a given service.

People must be given opportunities to express their worship to God in singing, giving, reading of Scripture, and hearing the preached word of God, and prayer. But sometimes the wind of the Holy Spirit will shift to accomplish the heart of God for His people. If we are going to indeed worship God in Spirit and in truth, we must be prepared to yield our plans, goals, and worship objectives to the leading of the Spirit.

When I am focused and hard after the directives of the Holy Spirit, all my energy, and my gifts are poured out in the direction of the Lord. I am still aware of the expectations of the people, but I am also subject to the wise counsel of the Spirit of God. Just as Mary did when she entered a room filled with important men. Mary had to decide who the most important person in the room was, and then what she would do about it. She entered a room filled with traditional mindsets, while caring in her heart unconventional inspiration. She came in to a place where she, a woman, was not invited, and she evidently was late because the meeting had already begun. With all eyes fastened on her, Mary seemingly disregarded all protocol. She pressed passed all the distractions, bringing with her an expensive gift. It was as if no one else existed or really mattered. Her priority was to get at the Master's feet and give to Him her expensive gift and her glory (Mark 14:3).

We as true worshippers should find this place in the Spirit, where we would be able to worship without restrictions, reservations, or fear.

In the Spirit, the priority is pleasing God, and everything else is secondary.

In the Spirit of God is also being in the presence of God. It is the eternal zone, a dimension reserved for Spirit beings. In the Spirit, John saw the Son of God, angels, thrones, elders, beasts, and so much more. John heard trumpets, heavenly music, and the sound of God's own voice. He spoke with angels and even tried to worship one. While in the Spirit, I too have seen spiritual beings, both angels and demons alike. I've heard heavenly sounds, and new music. God speaks to me and I'm able to hear His voice much clearer than when I am in the flesh. When I'm in the Spirit I feel closer to God than at any other time in my life.

I suppose that's because I am not in "time" when I am in the Spirit. I lose track of time and it becomes irrelevant compared to where I am and what I'm experiencing in that place. When we are in the Spirit, we are in the eternal zone. The eternal zone is the place where real freedom occurs. The Bible says "…where the Spirit of the Lord is there is liberty." (2 Corinthians 3:17).

Music has a way of transporting a listener to another place, thereby escaping the present woes. Praise music will certainly transport one into the presence of God. Always remember that escaping your present woes does not change them, but it most certainly will change you. You will begin to see things through your spiritual eyes, as God sees. You can rise to a place where you see things in the correct perspective. View your problems from God's standpoint. Let your fear be transformed into faith. I hope that as you have sung along with these songs that you've been transported to a heavenly place. Go to a place where you can escape the overwhelming realities of this life. I call this place my "Hiding Place".

Hiding Place
by Curtis L. Butler

Chorus:

Thou, oh Lord, are my hiding place
A shield in the time of war
Thou, oh Lord, are my hiding place
A shelter in the time of a storm
Thou, oh Lord, are my hiding place
A hiding place for me You are

Verse 1:

Just when I'm about to fall
You are there to sustain me
On Your name I would call
And You are there to protect me

Chorus:

Thou, oh Lord, are my hiding place
A shield in the time of war
Thou, oh Lord, are my hiding place
A shelter in the time of a storm
Thou, oh Lord, are my hiding place
A hiding place for me You are

Verse 2:

I run to You for refuge
Under the shadow of Your wing will I hide

I look to You for my direction
And in Your Word I will abide
Tag:
You're my hiding place
You're my hiding place
You're my hiding place
You're my hiding place
Ending:
Thou, oh Lord, are my hiding place
A hiding place for me You are
A hiding place for me You are
A hiding place for me You are

Butler Ministries Resources

For current prices of any of the resources listed below, please visit our web page. A special discounted price, as a blessing from the ministry, is available to all who purchase all three CDs. **Creative works of art by Curtis Butler are also available through Caricatures Christian Artworks. Visit our web page for more information.

~ CDs ~

Eternal Sounds Compilation CD The carefully selected compilation of songs on this CD is found throughout the pages of this book, Eternal Praise. The purpose of these original pieces of music is to assist the reader in singing the songs written within the pages of each chapter of this book (for your convenience, the list of songs & their chapter numbers is given below). Water the words you read with praise and worship as the Holy Spirit inspires you. Play the music in the background as you settle back to read, and maximize your experience as God speaks to you right where you are. Let these eternal sounds surround you with inspiration and exaltation.

Original Songs in This Book
- He Reigns ~ Introduction,
- Worship You ~ Chapter 1.
- Eternal Praise ~ Chapter 2
- Sacrifice ~ Chapter 3
- Jehovah-Shammah ~ Chapter 4
- Be Pleased ~ Chapter 5
- We Praise Your Name ~ Chapter 6
- Praise is a Weapon ~ Chapter 7
- Bless the Lord ~ Chapter 8
- My Everything ~ Chapter 9
- Everything That Has Breath ~ Chapter 10
- Victory ~ Chapter 11
- Hiding Place ~ Chapter 12

Eternal Praise CD - Get a copy of the CD project that compelled this author to begin his search into the eternalness of praise to discover the eternalness of God. Through a diverse style of music, these 12 songs will lead you, the listener, from praise, to worship, to prayer. Curtis Butler sings, with friends and family, these songs that were birthed through his own personal times with God. Some of these songs were recorded first on the Altar of My Heart CD and then re-recorded with the fresh sounds of live musicians. A brand new lift was given each song and will surely be a blessing to the listener.

Altar of My Heart CD - Experience the sounds that flowed from the psalmist's heart. Each song is an offering found on the altar of the writer's heart, set ablaze by fervent worship. These songs will make you dance, sing, and worship your way into the very presence of God.

About the Author

Curtis Butler is the worship and fine arts pastor at the Higher Praise Family Church, located at 2909 Horton in Forest Hill TX. Pastor Butler, his wife Laura, and their three children have served and grown there under the leadership of Sr. Pastor, Patrick McGrew, Sr. for over 10 years. Curtis studied music at Midland Jr College, and Art Education at Oral Roberts University. He is both a licensed minister of the gospel, and an ordained elder. Both Curtis and Laura have served as missionaries in the mountains of Jamaica, West Indies, Mexico, and El Salvador with Teen Mania Ministries, and in the Holy Land of Israel with Souled-Out Ministries. With worship and the Word of God, Curtis has traveled over many parts of the United States, spreading the good news of Jesus Christ in the demonstration of the power of God.

God has also moved through Curtis through his artistic contribution to the Kingdom of God. Curtis Butler uses his artistic gifts to bring glory to God in visual format and as an evangelistic tool to enlighten others of the powerful love of God, which is at work among mankind.

Purchase the CD that features many of the songs referenced in the book at www.butlermwaa.org

www.ingramcontent.com/pod-product-compliance
Lightning Source LLC
Chambersburg PA
CBHW071709040426
42446CB00011B/1982